Donald G. MacRae was educated at Glasgow University
and Balliol College, Oxford. He has been university
lecturer in Sociology at Oxford, Professor of Sociology
at the University of Ghana and the University of
California (Berkeley), and Fellow at the Center for
Advanced Study in the Behavioural Sciences at
Stanford, California. He is currently Professor of
Sociology at the London School of Economics,
University of London. He has lectured and broadcast
widely in North America and Germany, and for more
than a decade edited *The British Journal of
Sociology*. His publications include *Ideology and
Society* (1961) and *Ages and Stages* (1972).

Modern Masters

Weber

Donald G. MacRae

Fontana/Collins

First published in Fontana 1974

Copyright © Donald G. MacRae 1974

Printed in Great Britain
for the Publishers Wm Collins Sons & Co Ltd,
14 St James's Place, London SW1
by Richard Clay (The Chaucer Press), Ltd,
Bungay, Suffolk

To Mairi and Helen
with love

Contents

Preface

In this little book I have approached Max Weber by indirection. To the centre of a maze there is no other path, and I believe that Weber indeed presents us with a maze. One of the disappointments about real mazes is that at their hearts there is often nothing. I do not however think this true of Weber, though there is in my view less than has often been believed to lie hidden there. But the maze and its contents have certainly been sufficient to make of Weber one of the master figures of the social imagination in this century.

In so short a treatment I have tried to avoid both too much apparatus of learning and, whenever possible, a German vocabulary, despite the fact that Weber's use of language is peculiarly difficult in all but two or three of his published works – and these exceptions were formal lectures. As a consequence I have deliberately employed metaphor in my exposition while trying not to do violence to Weber's thought. I hope the result may inform the curious about Weber as social scientist and even help some students by giving them a route map to a mind peculiarly inseparable from the problems of a particular life in a highly specific cultural situation. But I am well aware that about so various a scholar no finality can be attained.

My wife, for reasons I understand, has suggested that I should dedicate this book to the memory of J. N. Hummel. I have however chosen not to do so.

Highgate, 1973

D. G. M.

1   The Reputation

The German sociologist Max Weber died at about five o'clock on the afternoon of June 14, 1920. The day had been wet and when Weber's student Karl Loewenstein visited the Weber home on the Seestrasse in Munich he found the sick man alone. For a few minutes Loewenstein stayed by the bed, watching the last struggles of his teacher. Then he left. Weber's wife Marianne was elsewhere in the house, resting. Shortly after Loewenstein's departure Weber died, unattended and solitary. He was fifty-six years of age and he had occupied his professorial chair in Munich for only a few months. Had he lived he intended to spend his next term at the university lecturing on socialism.

His death was a late consequence of the influenza pandemic, which, starting in 1918, killed it is believed more people than died as casualties of the 1914–18 war. By 1920 the disease had indeed become less virulent, but throughout Europe a population still weakened by privation, food-rationing and the effects of blockade remained vulnerable. Weber's case was not untypical. The influenza he had contracted in the early summer turned to pneumonia, and pneumonia – before the advances of chemo-therapy in the 1930s – was usually fatal. Scholars, particularly original scholars in new and developing subjects, often ripen late. It has often been assumed that when Weber died he was on the threshold of a synthesis of the studies of his lifetime, but of this there can only be conjecture, not proof. Since his death his reputation has grown steadily, and his name is certainly far more widely known today than ever in his life-time. What is

the basis of this posthumous fame? At the level of popular repute, I suggest, four factors are involved.

The first of these is very vulgar. In the 1960s it was a
fashion among journalists and others to ascribe the
quality of 'charisma' to any public, dominant and attractive person in the worlds of politics, entertainment and
the arts. Thus John F. Kennedy, Kwame Nkrumah and
the Beatles were all said to be 'charismatic personalities'.
A kind of circular argument was employed either quite
overtly or in a concealed form which ran: 'X is an attractive figure in the public eye; therefore X has charisma;
what makes X publicly attractive is his charisma.
Charisma is at once proof, evidence and cause of certain
kinds of public success.' Of course this quality was not
ascribed to all public men equally, or at all. Kennedy –
and, by extension, his family – were very charismatic;
Kruschev much less so. By the 1970s charisma was no
longer a vogue-word. It was not claimed that Nixon,
Heath or Pompidou had charisma – and I don't think this
is primarily due to the fact that they were not Kennedy,
Wilson or Charles de Gaulle. We owe this usage of
'charisma' largely to Weber. Whether it involves a dis-
tortion of what he had to say we shall see.

What, however, should be remembered is that Weber
got the word from theology: to have charisma is to have
divine grace, the grace of God, something, as St Thomas
Aquinas said, 'supernatural bestowed on man by God'.
Charisma then is not part of the natural order, not part of
the material world nor the world of society. It comes
from without. What it is doing in the writings of a sociologist, concerned to understand so far as may be, by the
ordinary means and concepts of science and scholarship,
how people get along – or fail to get along – together is
a good question.

The second factor contributing to Weber's place as an
object of general awareness is to be found, at a slightly

more rarefied level, in a metaphysical entity called 'the Protestant ethic'. I am not, of course, saying here that this concept is at all metaphysical in the actual writings of Weber, but simply that it operates metaphysically in a good deal of modern thought. Thus it is not uncommon to find the rapid growth rate of the economies of Japan, Singapore and Hong Kong ascribed to the Protestant ethic – which in lands which have hardly known Christianity, far less Protestantism, is surprising. (In a rather more sophisticated form the successes of these fortunate eastern isles is ascribed to 'a functional equivalent for the Protestant ethic'. I am not sure that this is much better.) Again, I know a text-book of history, widely used in British schools, in which the industrial revolution of the eighteenth century is explained by reference to the Protestant ethic of parsimony and diligence whereby both capital was accumulated and technological discovery induced. This is surely as metaphysical as the explanation offered in Molière's play *Le Malade Imaginaire* that the somnolence resulting from opium is caused by the dormitive principles in poppies. To these matters also we return later.

A third factor is the impact made on those who frequent libraries by the grim bulk of Weber's writings, writings which are composed in a style found difficult even by native German speakers and translated very often into either an English more obscure than the original, or into that extraordinary kind of French in which German nouns are borrowed – '*le historischer Kausalzusammenhang*', for example. From these ranked volumes there emerges an atmosphere of prestige and oppression typical of much German nineteenth century scholarship. The achievement of the German mind in the world of learning is a genuine one; but it is also very forbidding. Weber is part of it. His books are, particularly if they are not read, redolent of obscurity, knowledge and a promise of revelation. As a result Weber is seen as a kind of Magus.

And there is an additional quality to these books which is at once mysterious and tantalising. Very largely they consist of materials put together after his death. Weber was a man of enormous scholarly ambition, sporadic and volcanic energy, and wide learning. As a result a great deal that he intended to complete, to fill out or refine was left in a kind of chaos of articles, treatises, schema, lecture notes transcribed by students, and so on. This is not said in criticism, for no man in our century expects to die at fifty-six and no man should be condemned merely for attempting in the intellectual sphere more than he can actually accomplish. But the result is infuriating: eloquence, close reasoning, aridity, distinction for the sake of distinction, learning and superficiality go together in his work. To consult Weber, therefore, is often somewhat like divination, like using a Tarot pack or the *I Cheng*. This does not necessarily harm a reputation and, given genuine eminence – and sometimes not even that – a reputation with this component is likely to give rise to another source of fame in the form of a learned industry of exposition, criticism, disputation and interpretation. Internationally there is today a flourishing Weber industry. I am afraid this little book is another contribution to it.

But the fourth factor behind Weber's popular reputation is the most important. If the outlook of the nineteenth and early twentieth centuries was essentially dominated by historical attitudes and methods, so that Darwinism is a historical biology and Freudianism a historical psychology, the late twentieth century is an age of sociology. In sociology Weber is canonised. He is an accredited 'founding father' of the discipline. He is an object not of scepticism nor utility, but of piety. Even his critics like Herbert Marcuse are often men under his spell. To many sociologists and most of the lay public he is the sociologist *par excellence*. It is very hard to think of a parallel case: a Marshall or a Keynes in economics, a Malinowski or a Radcliffe-Brown in anthropology, a Planck or an Einstein in physics are, of course, great historical names in their subjects. A student, a researcher or a practitioner may gain refreshment, insight and knowledge from returning to them; but their work has been winnowed and absorbed into their disciplines. Weber, on the other hand, is seen as more than this sort of figure. I called him a Magus: he is that, a living presence to professional sociologists as well as to the sociological laity, and a living authority, unexhausted. A parallel case might seem to be that of his great French contemporary, Émile Durkheim, but in practice they are very different. I, to whom Durkheim is by far the greater sociologist, know perfectly well that Durkheim is dead and a part of the chronicles of my discipline, and this is true for the sociological profession as a whole. But Weber is only now settling into some sort of perspective and only now being sifted through so that we may take from him what is valuable and useful and discard what is disproved, what is a false lead, what is muddle and what was always mistaken. The process is far from complete.

It is not as if Weber were a political prophet, the founder of a secular religion like Marx. I think, indeed, that he was more of an ideologist and is admired more for ideological reasons than is commonly supposed, but no one is or has been a Weberian in even the mildest of the senses in which one can say that someone is a Marxist. It is true that he is believed to be a great sociological diagnostician, a writer who can still tell us about the origins and the real essence of our industrial society and our dreadful, rewarding century. It is true that he is believed to reveal discomfiting and tragic tendencies in the movement of our society and our politics. It is true that he is in some ways typically and, both consciously and unawares, a revelatory German – and Germany is a great and still enigmatic fact for Europe and the world. Because of his perplexities and his clarities Weber is both a guide and a clue to the enigmas of Germany in his own time, to the subsequent Nazi period, and to undecided issues of power and action in the present epoch. His fame, then, is bound up with his ambiguities, with the unadmitted or unexpressed belief that properly deciphered Weber would be found to conceal on his person the keys to both a specific society and to modern society at large.

If I may employ a metaphor and a phrase which I have used before, sociology is a major form of human self-consciousness, a kind of imperfect looking-glass in which we may see reflected back the visage of society as Perseus in the Greek tale saw the face of Medusa, that face which directly confronted turned men to stone. Sociology both makes society clear and present to us and makes society bearable and subject to analysis by endistancing us from the stark reality of immediate apprehension. It is this quality which gives sociology a public power far beyond anything one might expect from the very limited, though still valuable, nature of its actual achievement. The works of Weber, edited and put together in such large measure after his death, with their combination of learned gravity and romantic unction, and above all with their inconclusiveness and their suggestive contradictions, fulfil almost perfectly one public conception, secretly shared within the sociological profession, of the sociologist.

This would not be so true were he not mysterious. His great contemporaries in sociology were all gifted with clarity. I do not mean by this that they are easy writers. It is very difficult to provide easy reading about what is hard in content – and society is not simple – and it is probably impossible to deploy an elegant accessibility in one's prose on a difficult subject if one is also original. But Pareto (1848–1923), Durkheim (1858–1917), Hobhouse (1864–1929) are never mysterious. They may be wrong, they may be absurd, they may deceive themselves by bad argument, but they are not obscure. One knows what their problems are; one knows what they believe to be solutions. They may astonish us by insight and ingenuity and baffle us by naïvety, but they lead us through labyrinths. Weber leads us into labyrinths with no Ariadne's thread to aid our return. One can see this either as a merit, claiming that life and society really are like that, and that no one else has penetrated so far; or one can see it as a proof of failure, that failure which, as it is the defeat of great strength and great effort, is more honourable than success. I must admit a prejudice here which the reader should keep in mind in what follows : I prefer success to failure in science and scholarship, and while I admit that society is obscure and labyrinthine – what else? – that admission only strengthens my desire for clear charts, even if they honestly reveal areas still unexplored and the existence of precipices and rock-falls.

Finally, if we live in a thought-world which has been sociologised, we have to face another facet of Weber – that of the paradigmatic and exemplary sociologist. For a whole series of reasons the reputation of Karl Marx has been reborn in a new form, the form of Marx as sociologist. I believe that this is error : that Marx neither was – nor in a very important sense intended to be – a sociologist. But that is not an opinion which is widely shared. To those to whom Marxism is a sociology Weber is the great antagonist. And since in all antagonism there is also complementarity, Marx and Weber as sociologists are seen as opposed twins, as archetypes. That error, at least, I hope these pages will correct.

2 The Life

Max Weber was born in the town of Erfurt in Thuringia on April 21, 1864. Thuringia has now disappeared
into the anonymity of the communist German Democratic Republic. But in 1864 it was a part of the Prussian
dominion, of that power which perplexed and haunted
Weber throughout his life. His family was defined by its
Protestantism. His father's ancestors were Lutheran
refugees from the Austrian empire who had gone to
Bielefield and become major cloth merchants. His
mother's family traced itself back to Wilhelm von
Wallenstein, a German who had served in the armies of
the great Gustavus Adolphus, 'Lion of the North and
Bulwark of the Protestant Faith'. The Wallensteins –
spelt Fallenstein in Swedish – became intellectuals of a
kind; school teachers or what in Scotland would be called
dominies. One of them, such was a common destiny
for a dominie, took to drink and deserted his Huguenot
wife. His son, G. F. Fallenstein, in turn underwent a
period of mental disorder, then became an apostle of
German romantic nationalism and 'folkishness' who,
after fighting Napoleon, joined the military police in the
occupied Paris of 1815 and, in the following year, became
a bureaucrat in Dusseldorf. In Paris this man added
to his romantic German nationalism and his hatred for
Napoleon an inconvenient attachment to the libertarian
ideas of the French Revolution. As a result he did not
advance in his profession in the suspicious world of the
restoration until in 1832 he became state councillor
Regierungsrat) in Coblentz. There in 1835 he married,
for the second time, Emilia Souchay whose daughter

Helene Fallenstein was to be the mother of Max Weber.

The Souchays too had behind them a record as refugees of conscience, for they were by origin Calvinists who had fled from Orléans after the revocation of religious tolerance to the Huguenots in 1685. In Frankfurt they became successful merchants with branches of their business in London and Manchester. Fallenstein did well financially from the marriage and in 1842 moved to serve the Prussian government in Berlin. But he did not succeed in his new job, and in 1847 he retired to Heidelberg. There he occupied himself with good works, and in moving in learned circles dominated by the historians Schlosser and his pupil Gervinus. This friendship was to be of importance to the young Weber's destiny.

Schlosser was an opponent of the new 'scientific' history created by Ranke. No history, he said, could be free from value-judgements and preconceptions arising out of non-historical considerations. The historian has the moral duty to judge men and events. History teaches not only itself but is also an ethical activity which forms the character of its students and of their public life. Gervinus, who was of the seven Göttingen professors dismissed for constitutionalism by the Hanoverian monarchy, took part in the liberal Frankfurt Parliament of 1848, championed a federal Germany and irreconcilably opposed Bismarck and the Hohenzollern imperiam. Weber was to wrestle, inconclusively, with the problems set by these scholars all his life. But the influence of Gervinus was to be more than intellectual : it was to affect the familial, the sensual and the psychological formation of Weber until the day of his death, for Gervinus lived on in the Fallenstein home after Fallenstein's death. He tried to seduce Helene, Weber's mother. He then tried to arrange a marriage for her with one of his students. She escaped to the home of her sister, wife of the historian Baumgarten, in Berlin, and there she met and married Max Weber *père*. She never overcame her dread of the sexual life, and the marriage was one of unhappiness, pietism and complaint.

The man she married was the youngest son of the Biclefeld family, born in 1836. His eldest brother transformed the cloth business by instituting a rationalised putting-out system and flourished mightily as entrepreneur. The youngest brother, by training a lawyer, became after taking his doctorate both a civic employee and a journalist in Berlin. He was an ardent monarchist and Bismarckian. He went to Erfurt as a magistrate and then, after the birth of his son, came back to Berlin to pursue a minor but successful career in Prussian politics. Commentators have described his opinions as liberal : in no country but Hohenzollern Prussia could agreement with Treitschke or men like him be taken as a proof of liberalism. Yet the error about the politics of Max Weber *père* is in one way comprehensible. Imperial Germany developed no genuinely conservative party. The new Empire was always in some ways a power wherein legitimacy could not flow from the wisdom of the past, be a continuation of the *mos maiorum*. The Bismarckian 'National Liberals' to whom the elder Weber attached himself defined politics by the state, not society, and their state was the established order of Prussia. This was, as we shall see, by no means the same thing as the established order of the new, unified Germany.

Nor was Weber's father merely *l'homme moyen sensuel*, even if that is how his wife saw him. He was a part of that new nineteenth century world of newspapers and journals, of the politics of large franchises and narrow powers, of gossip, news and knowledge of what went on in the corridors of power – of parliaments, of government offices, of party headquarters, of newspaper administrations, and of a court. His moral principles were those of an 'ethic of success', not of intrinsic merit. The dichotomy was to haunt the son, but as a young man he followed his father's judgement. The father's circle was intellectual in a narrow sense: professors of history counted for much in it, but a concern with creativity, with beauty, with criticism as a torturing passion, with novelty, were not part of it. This world of Rickert, Sybel and Treitschke was intellectual, but also philistine. In it Weber's father would bear nothing pushed to extremes, no public reasoning, no course of action followed to the end: he was a man much at ease in Zion; publicly complaisant and privately demanding, expecting much of others. In this expectation neither father nor son, each in his own way, was greatly to be disappointed.

To all this Helene Fallenstein-Webber was opposed. Sex, we may feel, was as so often her weapon in the war of the sexes. If Marianne Weber, Max's wife, is to be believed her mother-in-law Helene hated sexuality: the marriage-bed was a place of sorrow and of sin. Only procreation could justify that unison of bodies from which age would bring a merciful release. What this meant to the elder Weber one can, with sympathy, imagine. From 1876 on the relations of Weber's parents were those of an institutionalised estrangement. The picture is a familiar one to any student of the nineteenth century. As is usual in this picture the Webers had numerous children, and as is also usual in that age they were familiar with the deaths of children. Helene Weber used the frail health and the danger of death of her eldest son as a criticism and a weapon against a father who was also not to be forgiven for the death of an infant daughter.

Helene was devout in her own way. In the issues of religion her mind was decided. She sought God personally, not through rites or theology. She did not seek Him emotionally, but in a conduct of quiet, decisive religiosity. She was much moved by that New England preaching of the nineteenth century which, etiolating Christianity and Calvinism, refusing the drama, the terror, the splendour and the order, advocated a resolved repudiation of emotion and desire combined with a narrow individualism and the finding of uncomfortable duty in the daily round. In a way this goes back to an old theme, influential in Britain and America, developed by Calvinists in the seventeenth century and to be found at work in the shorter catechism of the Church of Scotland – but not, I think, in either Calvin or in Knox. It is the idea that the sanctification of the individual is a process exemplified in the dutiful collaboration in God's work practised by the unfallen Adam in Eden and, after the Fall, offered to those who work in their calling by the Covenant of Grace. But to Helene Weber, reading the divines of nineteenth-century America, this teaching was cut from its roots, humanised, quietised and rationalised by two hundred years of history. It was powerfully to affect the thinking of her son.

When Helene had run off from Heidelberg to Berlin she took refuge as a seventeen-year-old girl with her elder sister Ida whose husband, Hermann Baumgarten, was to be yet another influence on the young Max. Baumgarten was an enemy of exactly those things and men to which Max Weber senior was much attached. He thought nothing of the eloquent, vulgar and moving Treitschke, and, in criticising Treitschke, he criticised by implication Prussia and the Hohenzollern dynasty. He had believed, like all his generation, in a unification of the German states, but not in the unification that he found. His attitudes, carried into the period after 1871, were largely those of Gervinus. Baumgarten therefore withdrew from the political order to preach a history conducted without party zeal and to condemn the Bismarckian empire as both unstable and unwise in its cults of war and power and its rejection of any true parliamentarianism. A non-political attitude of this kind, publicly expressed, is of course itself a kind of politics.

Weber's aunt, Ida Baumgarten, took a religious position close to that of Helene Weber, but unlike Helene she was an overtly dominant person in her home. She exercised an obtrusive charity, proclaiming the primacy of Christian duty. Weber was to find in her home both a puzzle and a challenge at a crucial period of his career when, as a conscript, he was stationed in Strasbourg, the capital of German-occupied Alsace. The politics and the religion of the Baumgartens were incorporated in the antinomies of his thought as a young man. Yet in a sense they had been present throughout his childhood. Not all the currents of Germany flowed into his early life – the workers and the nobles were not there – but there was enough in this materially comfortable, intense yet philistine milieu, to make him a man caught for ever in a net of inherited and contemporary contradiction. His sociology is, among other things, the record of his attempt to escape that net.

Let us now look at the formal facts of his career. They appear simple enough. At the age of two he was ill – undoubtedly very ill, though one may doubt the diagnosis of meningitis – and became the particular object of his mother's brooding concern. In 1869 the family re-settled in Berlin in the Charlottenburg district and Weber went to school there, receiving an orthodox, mainly classical education. In 1882 he went to Heidelberg and entered the law faculty. In 1884 he was at Strasbourg as a (conscript) junior officer. In 1884–5 he was at Berlin as a student, and 1885–6 at Göttingen. (In the German university system there was nothing unusual in this story of movement from place to place.) After leaving Göttingen he spent over three years holding a minor legal position in Berlin, preparing his doctoral

thesis and returning briefly as a reserve office to Strasbourg (he also served in the same capacity in Posen).
He took his doctorate with a thesis *On the History of
Medieval Trading Companies* in 1889. He was now an
'assessor' in the lower courts of Berlin. In 1891 he quali-
fied as a university teacher with a thesis on *The Signific-
ance of Roman Agrarian History for Public and Private
Law*. (It was at the examination of this thesis that the
great historian Theodor Mommsen said, 'When I
must descend to the grave I would happily say to no
one but the highly to be esteemed Max Weber, "My
son, here is my lance which is become too heavy for my
arm."') In 1892 Weber got a minor position in law-
teaching in Berlin and, in the same year, married his
second cousin on his father's side. In 1894 the University
of Freiburg-im-Breisgau gave him a chair in political
economy. In 1897 he succeeded the economist Knies at
Heidelberg. A 'nervous breakdown' followed, and in 1899
he was given leave to recover himself. He travelled in
Europe – England, Scotland, Belgium, Italy – and the
United States. In 1903 Weber with Sombert and Jaffe
found the journal, *Archiv für Sozialwissenschaft und
Sozialpolitik*. During the 1914–18 war he worked in
hospital administration. 1918 saw him return to teaching
in a specially created chair of sociology in Vienna. In 1919
he took over the chair previously held by another famous
economist, Brentano, in Munich. He died the following
year. Except for the prolonged 'breakdown' it is a
typical enough story of academic life, but that excep-
tion is a large one. One can only admire and perhaps
approve that element in the German university system
which allowed a man, however distinguished and intellectually productive, to abjure teaching for twenty years.

Before we look more closely at the personal life three
attachments should be mentioned, attachments at once
academic and political. One of these was to the Evan-

gelical Social Union (*Evangelischse-Soziale Verein*), a Protestant body which represented something of the same
reaction to industrial and urban society in its birth-
pangs which Christian Socialism and its successors in
England and, even more closely, the Social Gospel Movement in the United States, also characterised. The Union
was concordant in its views with the attitudes of his
mother and of the Baumgartens. It was an attempt to
make faith and charity relevant by social welfare and
social administration to a transformed society. Weber
was a founding member from 1890 onwards, and through
his membership became associated with the politician
and publicist Friedrich Naumann.

Older and more distinguished (it dated from 1872) was
the Social-Political Union (*Verein für Sozialpolitik*), one
of the most important of all the learned societies in the
history of the social sciences. In its early days the Social-
Political Union advanced views on social policy, but
from 1881 and the Bismarckian provisions in the field of
social assurance it concerned itself not with propaganda
but with research and discussion among academics. For
nearly all of Weber's period of membership (1888–1920)
the dominant figure in the Union was Gustav Schmoller
who, on the whole, steered its concerns away from technical and theoretical economics and kept its sights on
an approach, by way of social and economic history, to
questions of society. The Union was a spur to the early
researches of Weber and a platform for his opinions and
polemics. It would be absurd to regard the Union as
non-political after its change of policy in 1881, for its
researches were guided not by disinterested science, by
problems arising from the inner development of the
social sciences, but always by issues of public choice,
alarm or decision. I do not mean that this was somehow
through unconscious choice and interest: it was direct
and deliberate.

Thirdly there was the National Liberal Party. Though certainly national, the liberalism of this body might not have been recognised elsewhere in Europe. It was the party of the elder Max Weber who was a member of both the Prussian Diet and the imperial parliament or Reichstag. In religion as politics, Weber was always ambiguous. For all his concern with questions of faith and Christian charity he was, as he put it, 'religiously unmusical'. About political parties he was positively slippery, and not one feels merely from a desire to maintain an academic and poised objectivity. His doubts about the National Liberals are evident even when he was only twenty-three. Yet to the problems of German politics he constantly brought National Liberal attitudes so that, for example, he could support – yet ambiguously criticise – the National Liberal's acceptance of Bismarck's anti-socialist laws. Even in the sudden liberation of defeat from 1918–20 the ambiguities and the attitudes remain, even though he appears to be, at the last, politically committed as man and citizen. One can ascribe, if one wishes, a great deal of Weber's political flirtations – not so much adultery as adulteration – to both the real difficulties of his time and place and, secondly, to the scruples of a mind delicately aware of all the threads and tugs of consideration that are the web of politics. It seems to me, given those matters on which he was clear and unambiguous, that this is to do him altogether too much justice. And of course we should remember that some of such blame as there is does not really belong to Weber, but to those writers who since his death have worked to make him a modern master not only of thought and learning, but of political attitude and action.

3   The Man

The man who lived out his life in the tangle of family influence, public affairs and academic work is curiously elusive. Even about his mature physical appearance there are puzzles. He was tall, burly, heavily bearded and appeared stern. His speech, we are told, was simple and direct, yet also flexibly geared to the personality he was addressing. He is always pictured full-face, and I have been told – truly or not I cannot tell – that he objected to any representation in profile which might reveal the conformation of his nose. For his face was scarred from duelling accidents, and his features made heavy by much beer-drinking in his student days – his mother slapped his face on first seeing her coarsened son on his return from university. Weber gave an impression of poise, confidence and earnestness, but also, to a sensitive observer like the psychiatrist and philosopher Karl Jaspers, of contained tension, embodied schism.

There is, I have long felt, some justice in the idea of Wilhelm Reich that character is a coat of mail donned by men in our civilisation as a defence against the impulses of desire, of attraction and repulsion. This armour is itself a kind of social and historical product, and is not only a protection but also a pre-requisite for some kinds of aggression. If we take this metaphor seriously then Weber wore an armour of character which was both unusually heavy and restricting and unusually irksome to the tender flesh within. Weber's carapace was certainly so chafing, so ponderous that at times he found it unbearable.

His sensual and aesthetic life was restricted. He drank

and duelled as a student in the Corps of the Alemanni. At the same time, his wife tells us, he remained chaste. His first love affair with one of the Baumgartens seems sad, tepid and pure. His marriage with his relative Marianne Schnitzer was perhaps never consummated, and he wrote to her both of his constant struggle to endure and to domesticate his 'elemental passions' and also of his 'natural sobriety' as something which unfitted him for love. Not surprisingly he had a number of sentimental friendships with women throughout his life. But in his later years when he moved in more bohemian circles, intellectual rather than academic, he appears to have enjoyed a releasing and happy affair. (Again I have been told, but do not know how accurately, that he went to the Vienna chair towards the end of the war, not for the intellectual reasons which are suggested by most writers but to be near a new love.) Weber was deeply involved with his brothers and perhaps in some of his concerns we can find a certain substitute for paternity. There is to me something odd in the inter-marriage and inter-breeding of the academic and bourgeois clan to which he belonged – a pattern to which he contributed by his own marriage.*

The aesthetic world was one to which his relation remains puzzling. As a boy he is said to have steeped himself in the Greek and Roman classics; but their influence, save as source materials for economic, legal and (rarely) political study, is not apparent. Like all good Germans he knew his Goethe – and disliked his aesthetic hedonism – and he praised Schiller. But German literature seems hardly to have touched his young mind as an active influence. Of his great near-contemporaries we can find him, unsurprisingly, casting dilemmas into forms and

---

*Such clans are to be found in most countries. They form distinct sub-cultures and do much to further their members' careers in the higher education apparatus. Their dynamics deserve study.

situations derived from Ibsen, the greatest of all dramat-
ists of the protestant ethic. And we know that Nietzsche
powerfully influenced him, particularly in the last fifteen
years or so of his life, but I can see no sign that his
influence had any aesthetic reasonance such as it undoubtedly had on Weber's brilliant contemporary in
German sociology, Georg Simmel. In the great age of the
arts which was to flower most fully in the German-
speaking lands after 1918, but which begins in the 1890s,
Weber moves blindly even when he is associated with
the circle around the symbolist poet Stefan George –
about whom Simmel wrote and who was admired by
Weber even before they had met. It is indeed understandable that Weber was not at home in this anti-
academic hot-house of sometimes perverse emotion and
individual adulation, yet the release of spirit so evident
in his later years clearly owed much to these stumbling
contacts. His aesthetic incapacity seems to me both willed
and inherited: willed as inappropriate to the serious-
ness and depth of the scholar, inherited as a consequence
of the pietism and philistinism of his family background.

I do not know how far he was a man for whom the
visual world existed. His travel letters from Scotland, for
example, are full of conventional appreciations of land-
scape, but it is a mistake to think that conventional
responses are necessarily either false or mistaken. His
writings on music are learned and suggestive, but unusually obscure and related to what is perhaps the central
theme of all his thought, the rationalisation, secularisation and de-mythologising of the human world. One
would not need to care for music to write thus, but
to *choose* to do so is surely significant.

These matters may seem remote from a concern with
Weber's central interests. Yet if I am right about him
they are in fact very relevant. Durkheim in France so

defined his sociological concerns that the emotive, sensual and aesthetic spheres are not central to his effort at an understanding of how society is possible. Weber's strategy, however, should permit no such exclusion, and as a result his defects and rejections in these sectors of existence both flaws his total achievement and puts much of it in question. Yet as so often one feels a contained tension, an unstated polarity in all he does, exactly here. We are close to his essential enigma.

No one has written of Weber without talking of tension, of unresolved, perhaps agonising contradictions. Could he have found relief in action rather than in study and in thought? Throughout his life he recurs to his capacity for a *vita activa*, the merits of and the need for such a life. Yet he always draws back from it until his fiftieth year. He dramatises this need throughout his life, but it seems mere dramatisation until 1914. Many dons go on like this; discontented with the *vita contempliva* they express themselves violently and curse the *accidia* which is the occupational disease of their trade. Certainly Weber enjoyed himself hugely in his work as an administrator of nine major and forty minor hospital units during the war. He drove his car – known as the 'yellow peril' – furiously from place to place, and his duties delighted him and were well performed. He conventionally regretted not being a fighter – he seems quite to have enjoyed and to have valued his military service and his role as reserve officer – and expressed the extraordinary wish that the war had not come twenty-five years earlier, which, he contended, would have been the right time for it. (One can only ask, why?) His fascination with power and force, common enough in the Europe of his day, still seems excessive and sickly. Action may well discharge tension: but is tension always something that is best discharged?

All of which takes us to the nature of the prolonged

'break-down'. The young Weber worked prodigiously hard. His academic output down to 1893 is enormous in learning, range and volume. True he was financially secure, but he both resented his financial dependence on his family and was extremely ambitious for academic and public advancement. His early work is therefore both scholarly and directed to issues of public policy, above all the agrarian problems of Prussia's eastern marches, the world of the Junkers and of the subordinate Slavs. And in these years he was changing his domestic allegiances. To put it crudely he was changing from being his father's to being his mother's son. The worldly, compliant and relaxed father who appeared in public was something of a domestic tyrant who suffered from the fact – not in itself surely without reward – that his earnings did not equal his wife's inherited income. We have mentioned their sexual incompatibility, but there was beyond that a disdain for his wife's pieties and charity. It is difficult not to believe that the father represented not just a domestic despotism but also the imperial state, philistine and bullying, of which he was a pillar. The attitudes of Max Weber, at once admiring, obedient and dissident, to the German state, surely reflect and continue his attitudes to his father. At the same time he longed for the reform or ending of that state, yet found in it an admirable strength.

The elder Max Weber died in 1897 and the period of the son's breakdown followed. One is inclined to use an old piece of jargon and say that it is no accident that Weber's sociology and political thinking recur again and again to the themes of patriarchalism, patrimonialism and authority. To use a necessary argot, he attempted to internalise in his own personality those strong qualities of the German state which he both admired and dreaded, and those moral commitments, severed from the tree of religious life, which were the core of his mother's being. For perhaps seven weeks before the father's death he and his son had been locked in dispute. The quarrel was a family one: should the father live in Heidelberg with his wife and son? The desire does not seem surprising and the quarrel disproportionate. Anyhow, shortly after his father's funeral Weber became ill, apparently recovered and did some lecturing for the Evangelical Social Union, but by May 1898 became insomniac, walked weeping in the spring woods and was hospitalised. From then on brief recoveries, with the torture – as he found it – of teaching, followed in a deepening succession. His mother, in the Calvinist tradition, was unimpressed: her son should 'pull himself together'. In 1900 he began a leave without terminal date from the university.

For three years he travelled in Europe. In 1902, however, he felt able once again to read and to work, even if lightly, and in 1903 he undertook along with Werner Sombart the editorship of a learned journal, the *Social Science and Social Political Archives*.* In 1904 he visited America, on an invitation to the Universal Exposition at St Louis, travelling as far as Oklahoma and New Orleans, impressed everywhere by the force and the brutality of American capitalism and a political order in which the concomitant of democracy was machine politics, city bossism, and efficient, bureaucratic party organisation. In these years of 'breakdown' he now wrote furiously out of an extended knowledge and concern for the world. He was becoming truly a sociologist, not a jurist nor an economist, and by 1909 he was publicly commited to sociology as a discipline and to membership of the new German Sociological Society (*Deutsche Gesellschaft für Soziologie*), a body of active and committed scholarship under the presidency of the venerable Tönnies. Yet officially he was still an invalid and, though

*Archiv für Sozialwissenschaft und Sozialpolitik.

his world and health expanded in the immediate pre-war years to include new friends and new concerns, his liberation from the burdens of a wounded mind really begins only with the war of 1914 and becomes complete with the fall of the Empire in 1918 and with Weber's final desertion of his monarchist principles. The death of the state may be said to have completed the cure of a malaise precipitated by the death of his father.

One should not view the years from 1904 onwards as a time of mere hypochondria. In the few letters in Weber's own tiny, crabbed hand which I have personally examined from this period one finds his difficult script becoming more obscure and irregular just as he himself and those who wrote about him report fresh attacks and recurrences of ill-health. Yet there is a sense in which the illnesses and hypochondrias, the mysterious ailments and nervous crises which an earlier stage of medical science so freely permitted its more prosperous patients, were protective. Today we might well set about curing a Carlyle, a Herbert Spencer, a Charles Darwin, a Max Weber: as a result we might also make their mature work impossible. Illness is no longer a licit defence against the importunities of the world knocking at the door of the artist or scholar. We have become puritanical about health: to be ill, which was then an alternative vocation for the comfortably off, is now a source of guilt and even of condemnation. One cannot go back and diagnose Weber, though certain hypotheses seem inescapable, but it does appear likely that without his breakdown we would not have or know, even in its fragmentary form, the work to which he owes his present fame and influence. The strength of the German academic system that could allow Weber his prolonged leave, his 'titular' chair, his ambiguity of field – he can be thought of as lawyer, historian, economist, philosopher, political scientist as well as sociologist – is today nowhere to be found. In it Weber could take advantage of his real sufferings and turn them to the advancement of learning.

He had one other advantage in his relative financial security. The dynamics of his clan, with its intermarriages, consolidated rather than dispersed family capital in a world of stable currencies and low taxation. The private scholar – and that is what Weber in part was – could flourish modestly in the Europe of the nineteenth and early twentieth century. The institutionalised and bureaucratic research of our age has almost no place for him. The economies of our time, so much richer in so many ways, hardly permit such an existence. To ask, as I have heard it put, for a new Max Weber to redeem modern sociology, is to ask what is institutionally, economically and culturally impossible in the Europe of the late twentieth century. Weber was, as is true of us all, but was particularly true of him, a man of his time and society; not merely because he unavoidably embodied and expressed something of the spirit of his age, but because he lived in a Europe which specifically permitted his individual style of life and work.

4   The Country

The most remarkable thing about Weber's Europe is that it was at peace and remained so for forty-three years after the signing (in the Swan Hotel in Frankfurt) of the treaty which brought to an end the Franco-Prussian War. Of course the powers of Europe waged wars in other continents; of course and in particular in south-eastern Europe there were wars and revolts in which the greater powers intervened. But there was no war which engaged the major powers against one another. If much of the responsibility for the outbreak of war in 1914 must lie with the German Empire, it is equally true that it was that Empire which had by diplomacy, threat and ingenuity done much to maintain the longest peace Europe has known in the history of its state system. German arms had created a new Europe; the fear of these arms helped to maintain it.

The German state was very odd, and there has been nothing quite like it before or since. It is this oddity that makes Weber in my judgement less significant as a political thinker than is usually believed or than he might have been. The other new polities of his age, the Third French Republic and the Kingdom of Italy, are full of political instruction for any student of modern representative government, and if that instruction is not always edifying it is very human, and thus valuable. But the German state was a mish-mash; it was at once a dynasty, a federation, a representative system, a despotism, an army, a bureaucracy and a colonial regime. The dynasty of the Hohenzollerns did not possess a separate historical dignity like the Hapsburg *domus Austriae*, but it was nonetheless of great weight for the dynasty had powers and loyalties which were large, if ill-defined. It was possible, it was even usual, for men like Weber to approve the monarchist principle and condemn the monarch who was at once Emperor, Commander-in-Chief and King of Prussia and open to criticism in all three roles as well as personally. The federation too was a reality, not a façade, but the will of Prussia was its core and Prussia could out-vote all the rest of the federation's members. In it the three free northern ports, the seventeen dukedoms and the other three kingdoms possessed real but subordinate wills. Weber's mind moved always in the orbit of the dominant, Prussian, will.

The representative system is too complex for its exploration to be worth space in an account of Weber, even though Weber loved to play at constitution making. The constituent states typically were bi-cameral, with an aristocratic upper house and a lower chamber elected by universal manhood suffrage. In Prussia the three tier electoral regime kept power in the hands of the landowners and men of the right. The imperial parliament (*Reichstag*) stood ambiguously to the Chancellor of the Empire who could claim to be responsible not to it but to the Kaiser. The army estimates were indeed renewed by the *Reichstag* but only every seventh year, so that the Chancellor had a motive for alarm and bellicosity at regular intervals. Yet all in all Kaiser and Chancellor were despotically situated in relation to the legislative and executive powers of the state. To the army, the most powerful force in all that world, their will was central. Every man was a soldier and thus a subordinate in the one formative role which attached him to the one certainly national and glorious institution of the society. How far was he also a citizen? Weber was hardly to examine this situation. One must assume that he accepted it and its consequences.

The German state was, of course, a bureaucracy. The fame of that civil service, orderly and efficient is very great. Yet it was not unique, and Austria-Hungary, with less fuss, had a very loyal and efficient bureaucracy. Similarly it is a commonplace that the continuity in the history of the French state is the continuity of its administrators; and the imperial Indian Civil Service probably did more, better, with smaller resources than any other bureaucracy in history. Yet somehow it is assumed that the civil services of the German empire were peculiarly exemplary. Certainly these services regulated more things in more detail than in other lands; and Weber never questioned the paradigmatic character of the system, while his fellow-countrymen accorded it a respect and an obedience to be found nowhere else in Europe. What is more, it was only in imperial Russia that so wide a range of professions and vocations were included within the categories of public service. Elsewhere societies were more diverse and centres of countervailing power were to be found in a complex of associations and free professions. Through the army and the bureaucracy the state in Germany extended uniquely far into the fabric of ordinary life. Weber's reputation rightly depends in large measure on his work as diagnostician of the bureaucratic order. His opportunities for undertaking a clinical study of bureaucracy, where the state through its administrative, apparatus claimed such omnicompetence, were uniquely great.

In its eastern and western marches Germany was a colonial power. Alsace-Lorraine was a *Reichsland*, an area of imperial administration. (A destiny which Weber thought during much of the war perfectly suitable for a good deal of conquered western Europe.) In the east the Prussian heritage to Germany of largely Slav territories ruled by landed aristocracy, depending too on immigrant non-German labour, represented an older kind of colonialism. How could the Empire do with or do without these non-Germans, peasants and coal-miners? Could Prussia exist without its eastern lords, those Junkers who in large measure *were* Prussia, but who ruled and exploited these non-Germans? Here was a contradiction in the heart of the ideology of the empire: its claims to legitimacy were largely those of common speech and blood, of national self-determination, of 'folkishness', but Prussia, the major constituent of the empire, was a regime of caste and of rule over aliens. Weber's career as sociologist emerged directly out of his engagement with these problems.

Weber was strictly and in both the Marxist and non-Marxist senses a bourgeois, a man of the upper, trading orders of urban life. The world of the soil and the world of the aristocracy were alien to him. The world of the latter was the dream of the bourgeoisie: Germans had made no 'Declaration of the Rights of Man and the Citizen', they had indulged in no Putney Debates, far less executed anointed kings. Walter Rathenau, Jewish industrialist, patriot and statesman, once told the German upper middle-classes that they would never dare to push their principles or their politics *à outrance* for they loved and feared a system in which one might oneself receive a patent of nobility, enter an upper chamber, or see one's son officially advanced. The aristocratic fact was a central source of the unpolitical politics of Weber's class. Ruthenau was right.

In such a regime the daily business of politics was inevitably stultifying, arbitrary, likely to run into the sands or be swept by whirlwinds. The political structure was too irrational, complex and arbitrary for either a healthy practice or a profound political science. Fears were magnified, hopes turned on individuals and hypotheses about individuals and situations, so that Germany was not a political laboratory such as Tocqueville had found in America, but a witches' cauldron from which even a Weber could derive only ambiguous prophecy, alarm, and a faltering, irresolute will.

But in no polity however authoritarian – and imperial Germany is not to be confused with the authoritarian states of modern times – is the state coterminous with the society. Weber's society may, regarded as a nation, have lacked a civic culture, but it contained in its constituent parts local traditions in which both civic culture and civic courage could be found. This localism was not favoured in the Empire, and it concerned Weber, a mobile member of the academic profession, very little. As a result his diagnosis of actual situations tended to extremes and to polarisations. What is more, Weber as a Protestant failed to properly appreciate that nearly 40% of the population were Catholics. Weber's extensive writings on religion in Europe and Asia start from a Protestant point of judgement and tacitly accept the proposition that the Protestant and the German spirits are one.

This belief was a commonplace of the age, but one we must remember when we look at what Weber had to say about Protestantism and capitalism. Not merely was the official ideology of the dynasty Protestant, but throughout America, England and Germany wealth, power and valour were supposed to be correlated with reformed Christianity. Sometimes this correlation was referred for explanation to some independent biological merit of the Teutonic peoples and sometimes Protestantism was itself regarded as the cause of wealth and power as well as being also their reward. Bismarck's struggle with the Catholic church in Germany, from 1871 to 1887, could be understood – and was understood – to be at once national and economically progressive. So Protestantism was at once sacred history and the wave of the future.

Progress was above all conceived to be economic. Although certain parts of the *Reich* had industrialised early in the nineteenth century, the empire as a whole was in the late nineteenth century a state moving into advanced industrial capitalism at break-neck speed. Only in the post-bellum United States could anything similar be found. The railway network was completed. The iron of Lorraine fed the new mills and factories. The French war indemnity provided a new source for investment. German industry was from its foundations large-scale and technologically advanced, and in fields like heavy chemicals it led the world. The great banks flourished in this situation of new demands and opportunities. Rationalisation was the order of the day: a single capital market – Weber was much interested in stock exchanges, making a special study of that in Glasgow – a single currency, a single system of weights and measures, and a single code of industrial and commercial law served and were served by the new order of rational gain. Corporations multiplied. Weber witnessed the creation of an industrial society.

And he saw also the creation of a new scale and style of urban life. The old, traditional Germany of petty towns and petty dignitaries, all linked to small trade and closely bound to rural markets and supplies was becoming a country of great cities – the very word *Grosstadt* was invented to describe them – of which Berlin with its four million inhabitants was the chief. By 1900 only about 20% of the Germans lived in country areas. These great cities were places of bankers, bureaucrats and traders, of skilled professions and clerks, but most of all they were the homes of a new working class. As the total population grew, surpassing that of England or France in numbers, although also significantly younger, this working-class increased disproportionately. It seemed as though the new cities were fulfilling the implied predictions of Marx not merely in moving into industrial capitalism, but in polarising Germany into two antagonistic sectors of which the workers formed the larger group. In thirty years the trade unions multiplied their numbers nearly ten times so that in 1914 they had over three million members. The socialists, persecuted by Bismarck, still grew in strength and represented, it appeared, radically new principles of party organisation so that radical hopes were carried forward by bureaucratic mass politics based on the towns. To come to grips with the city and its politics was therefore a central challenge to Weber's understanding of society. It is probably fair to say – and a judgement of the progress of the social sciences over the fifty years since Weber's death – that no one has better grasped the social nature of modern urbanism since his time.

Save in the military sphere where union was imposed and gladly accepted, German society in Weber's period presents a picture of incoherence and competing forces matched in no other European country. Nor were the jarring forces so locked that any kind of stability resulted; rather all was uncertain and shifting in the dynamism of enormous energy and ceaseless change which characterised Germany. That at the cultural level there were profound continuities was something that a century of often terrible history has taught us, but the importance and inertia of these cultural factors were things inevitably invisible to Weber's generation. Indeed, it seemed possible that men were being atomised, separated from their fellows, their society, and their past, and that only a fragmented mass would remain. In all this turmoil of growth there was a sense of an ending, a twilight beyond which lay what night, what dawn?

Bismarck himself wrote that in 'our parliamentary parties the real point of crystallisation is not a programme but a man, a parliamentary *condottiere*'. As early as the 1890s Weber saw in the rootless middle classes and the fragmented masses a 'longing for a new Caesar'. The peace lasted forty-three years, but these years were felt to be precarious, and it is surely not too fanciful to find in Weber's nervous questing, his raids, often in depth, into so many territories of the mind, a reflection not of his character alone, but of the perplexities of his age and country. War or a new Caesar – or some union of the two – might at least give some ease to these frets in the resolution of obedience and sacrifice. But these possibilities in their turn raised new questions and new fears. Only the pace of change continued unabated and the fragmented world stayed for no answer.

5 The World of Learning

It was in the nineteenth century that knowledge became
an industry. It was in the German universities that this
industry was perfected. Knowledge is, of course, a social
and public enterprise. It depends not only on study and
discovery but also on criticism. For a subject to exist in
the world of knowledge there has to be a community of
scholars of that subject, communicating with each other,
judging by common standards each other's work. Knowledge is then, and on the whole, cumulative – though the
power of institutionalised forgetfulness in the world of
learning should never be underestimated. To be engaged
in the knowledge industry is thus to be involved in a
kind of progress. By way of learned societies, books and
journals, laboratories and libraries, teaching positions
allowing time for discovery and expecting publication
by their holders, learning becomes an institution of
society. Learning in a particular subject, and even the
advancement of knowledge, once that subject is institutionalised, does not demand talent, far less genius, so
much as orthodox labour. The labourers undergo a kind
of apprenticeship and, increasingly following the German pattern, are expected to produce, in its original
sense, a masterpiece – that is, a sample of decent
academic work as an entitlement, usually marked by the
conferring of the doctorate, to engage in advanced teaching and research. The process is very similar to that of
the craft-apprentice earning the right to full membership
of a master's guild.

Now sociology in the late nineteenth century, was not
– as it is now – institutionalised in this way. There was

not, except in America, and even there only in a rather thin form, a community of sociologists in university positions and proudly legitimated by an appropriate training. The subject had indeed a long and ragged history. Retrospectively but accurately the activities of Montesquieu in France and of Ferguson in Scotland could be called sociological. The word itself had been invented by Comte in France and he had worked out a programme for it and awarded the study of society a unique and privileged position as the crown of all the previously developed sciences. Few people had agreed. Neither the contents nor the methods of the enterprise were unambiguously defined. The activity of sociology was taken to be subversive in that it inevitably, by the mere fact of enquiry, questioned the existing state of social affairs. In the hands of Comte subversion went deeper, for to Comte sociology was not merely a study but a programme of reform – and as an ideology Comtean sociology had little popular or official appeal for Europe, though it was in fact to be politically influential in South America and elsewhere. What was more, the word 'sociology' was connected by many with socialism and the subject consequently condemned on the principle of guilt by association. The greatest nineteenth century sociologist, Herbert Spencer, was neither educated in a university, nor employed by one for all his ingenius and powerful defence of free market capitalism.

The first major work of German sociology appeared in 1887. Its author, Ferdinand Tönnies, lived most of his life without attaining to a university chair, yet *Community and Association* (*Gemeinschaft und Gesellschaft*) is still, rightly, read, and Tönnies is still a living influence on social thought. His younger contemporary, Weber, therefore was fortunate in that he gained academic advancement in other fields before becoming unequivocally committed to sociology, just as sociology as an institutionalised discipline has been fortunate in being able to claim for itself the legitimacy given by Weber's work and name.

History and the historical approach were the great German specialisms. German historians had established new canons of rigour in the use of sources, new standards of accuracy in exposition and new modes of barbarity in academic prose. Everything was viewed from the standpoint of history and it was believed that the central meaning of understanding was historical and developmental. To know the origins of a thing was to possess that thing. Thus law was to be grasped by the twin historical studies, firstly of Roman law and its European reception in the sixteenth century, and secondly by the yet more important study of the historical evolution of the legal customs and codes of the Teutonic barbarians and their medieval transformation. Again philology vindicated the historical method by researches which were both comparative and inductive as well as historical. Even economics in Germany was more and more made subject to history, at the cost of lagging far behind what was achieved in pure analysis in Britain, France and Austria, but with the gain of the construction of a viable discipline of economic history. The intellectual atmosphere breathed by the young Weber was saturated with history.

The achievement was genuine and great, and we are all in its debt. Weber belonged to what was probably the first European generation which could command with confidence a vast range of reliable secondary sources. True, these sources were mainly historical, but their accuracy, even as the mechanical products of the knowledge industry, was exemplary and their range enormous. Weber had good secondary sources not merely for the classical (primarily Roman) world and Europe, but also for his studies of China, India and ancient Palestine.

Nothing is more stupid or vulgar than to blame either Weber or subsequent sociologists for often relying on and making use of the projects and results of the industry of historical knowledge. After all, what else is that industry for?

I think, in fact, that there is more than one good answer to that question, but surely such a utilisation of these secondary sources is as good and legitimate as any other. No one expects a physicist or chemist to do each and every piece of research over again before using the results reported in the learned journals. Surely the human studies can proceed similarly, and Weber is to be rather envied than condemned for belonging to an age when such a utilisation of the work of others was possible. Two matters, however, are worrying. Weber was blind to an alternative approach to data which was developed by Spencer in England and advanced by Durkheim in France. Secondly, he was intoxicated by the detail of his sources and frequently bemused by a historical attitude of mind into a forgetfulness of his original purposes in embarking on a particular study. He was also unfortunate in my judgement – which on this matter is not widely shared – in getting involved in the German intellectual crisis about the nature and validity of historical knowledge itself.

The trouble here was a consequence of a sense that rigour in method was not enough, and that unless history could be shown to have foundations in accord with the criteria set by philosophy and logic then its claim to be even a valid form of knowledge – far less the most valid form – could not be sustained. If that claim fell then German historiography was devalued and the position of the other human sciences, all of which were supposed to be essentially historical, was put in the gravest doubt. These worries were compounded by a set of interlinked problems about values. Could a historian (or sociologist,

etc) avoid the intrusion of his own values into his work?
Should he do so? Even if he should and could do so in
his own specific work, must the very choice of an area
or problem for study not inevitably involve him in a
decision that demanded a valuation of problems one
against another? Even at the conscious level these could
seem grave issues, but there was worse.

The late nineteenth century has been called the age of
the discovery of the irrational and the unconscious. This
is not quite true: irrationality is an old issue for thinkers
and an older realisation of poets and story-tellers. The
unconscious has a long history, too; before Freud in the
German-speaking countries there had been the philo-
sophies of the unconscious of Schopenhauer and Hart-
mann. If, however, it was now recognised with a special
poignancy that all men, even scholars, were frequently
irrational in their behaviour and were moved by unconscious forces – implanted how in their being? – then did
it not follow that all sciences, but most particularly
perhaps the social sciences, were called in question? And
sociology itself also raised very sharply the possibility
that all scholarship was tainted, penetrated by values,
distorted by the very constraints and interests of social
life itself. Weber demanded of himself, at a time when
these things were widely felt but not yet always precisely formulated, rigorous answers to these issues, a
hard and unambiguous solution to these uncertainties.
How could a social science be established that was strong
enough to accept that a presuppositionless history was
impossible, and to deal rigorously with irrationality, unconscious motivation and the prompting of social interest?

That question has not yet been answered. We are in
the position of the legendary Presbyterian minister who
set out his sermon under numbered headings and who,
on coming to number four, said, 'And now, fourthly, we

come to a great difficulty. Let us look it firmly in the face and pass on. Fifthly, brethren ...' I am not sure that Weber, despite his wrestling with these difficulties, did much better. Nor, as I am hoping to show, am I sure that these difficulties, fundamental though they appear are either so important or so troublesome as Weber and his expositors and critics have believed. It is almost certainly not an illusion to believe that the bulk of the best and most original work in the physical and social sciences has been done by people who were either untroubled by problems of the foundation and methodological justification of their subject, or who turned only to such questions once their early passion for the specific and urgent in their subject had been slaked. No doubt such comforting counsel is very philistine, but it is unjust to assume that even philistines are always wrong.

What in fact saved Weber from drowning in a sea of intellectual and moral relativism was his passion for empirical knowledge. No one has ever accused him of lacking learning, and I know distinguished contemporary scholars who still read Weber precisely for the information which he makes accessible on such a wide range of subjects. Yet his historicism and perhaps his nationalism did cut him off from researches that would have proved useful and corrective in his work and from an approach which would, at the least, have enabled him to order it better. I don't want to suggest that Weber should have read more, but that it would have been better for him if he had read differently.

Despite the thick volumes of comparative ethnology which were produced in Germany, the Germans made a comparatively small contribution to what is now called social anthropology – what we may take here as being the sociology of contemporary primitive peoples. The best work in this field in Weber's day was British, French and American. No doubt the imperial successes of

England and France and the territorial expansion of the United States at the expense of the Indians had something to do with this, but the Germans had great travellers, zealous missionaries and something of an empire too. The Austrians after all, can be thought of as having done better than the Germans in this field, and they entirely lacked two of these attributes. What is certain is that Weber was ignorant here, and that the data of social anthropology would have simplified, corrected and altered his work. What is more Weber was negligent in his attention to a great predecessor and a greater contemporary.

I refer to Herbert Spencer and Durkheim, both of whom availed themselves of the new data of anthropology. Spencer was an evolutionist, not a historicist – that indeed is his weakness – but his analysis of society was based on certain timeless taxonomic principles: these are the concepts of social structure, of function, and of institution. Weber never got any of these clear. To him society is not overtly describable in terms of a structure of social relations which subserve certain ends – i.e. have functions – and which are ordered by institutional patterns. Such a structure can be viewed in a number of different ways, as for example one of relations between individuals, or as between groups, or as between the roles people play in society. Now with Spencer these possible alternatives are not spelled out but implied in a fairly commonsense mixture. Durkheim in his analysis of the forms of social solidarity was to do rather better. One of the influences on Durkheim was Weber's contemporary, Wilhelm Wundt. But Weber did not learn ahistorical (synchronic is a fashionable term) thinking from Wundt either. The richness of Weber is paid for in his exclusive historicism and a failure, which is not just one of clarity, but of understanding, to grasp the direction of the main line of sociological thought. Given the existence of Wundt one cannot ascribe this entirely to the understandable autarchy of late nineteenth century German scholarship. Ideally the sociologist should be a spectator and critic of the flux of time, not submerged in it or even – like the historians – victoriously embattled with it. Durkheim was perhaps the first man to realise this possibility.

On the other hand Weber drew on a rich and very largely German store of knowledge and ideas which was not used on any scale by his great contemporaries. This was the history of religious and critical theology. The primary works in this field were concerned with Judaism and Christianity, but its range was that of all that we now call 'the world religions', plus the religious systems of classical Greece and Rome. Here Weber read widely –British writers on Indian religion, Robertson Smith on the cults of the ancient Semites, a vast profusion of international studies of Confucianism and Taoism, and so on, as well as English and American sectarians, sources which are partly explicable in terms of his mother's highly personal form of late Calvinism. About religion, in a great age of scholarship, he is not parochial, although again one can feel it a pity that his knowledge of the best contemporary anthropological work was not greater. Had it been more extensive he might not only have concerned himself with the role of religion in the values whereby men act, but also have seen that the fundamental categories of our understanding, so often bound up with our conception of the sacred, are implicated in social structure. But in an area where he achieved so much there is perhaps something petty in such a comment.

Ultimately the fact is that no general sociologist can ever of himself know quite enough, even if he is a demon-driven polymath. In Weber's time and place there was only emerging a community of sociologists with at once a division of labour and common interests and standards. The institutionalisation of sociology was something to which Weber contributed both by his activity and his example. By doing so in both ways he helped to make of sociology that major form of our self-consciousness as social beings which it has become.

In all this I have been writing as though sociology had no quantitative aspect, as though indeed there was nothing to the popular image of the sociologist as simultaneously someone who pries into the affairs of his neighbours and yet is distanced from them by subjecting them to surveys and questionnaires which are then further removed from the untidy reality of affairs by being processed – preferably by computer. Of course, Weber had no computer – though the Austrian G. Hollerith had invented his data-sorting machine in 1894. Yet by Weber's time such research had had a long history and was well established, even though the use of sampling – an old tradition – only became formalised by such people as Bowley in the early twentieth century. Weber was well aware of such possibilities, but such studies contributed little to his major work and his contribution to such studies is not important.

Certainly he did produce early studies of agricultural labourers in East Prussia. And in 1907 Weber, under the influences of his brother, the cultural sociologist Alfred Weber, attempted a study of the effects of industrial life in large firms on the workers. He continued to be interested in such questions of industrial sociology, workers' attitudes and industrial psychology, and he also planned an abortive empirical research into the press and its effects. But only the early studies for the Social-Political Union and the Evangelical Social Union seem to me of any interest today. However, Weber certainly knew what was going on in the world of social surveys and statistics. As we shall see the one element of real value that he took from it is what we may call his 'probalistic' outlook.

Weber claimed that his intellectual milieu was dominated by Marx and Nietzsche, and that one could judge the members of that milieu very largely by the stand they took in relation to these towering personalities, so that anyone 'who does not confess that he could not do the most important part of his own work without these two deceives himself and others'. The role of Nietzsche in Weber's development and position, particularly in his latter years, has become a dominant theme in modern Weber scholarship. As for Marx, one of the most frequently recurrent questions set students of sociology in Britain and America is the request to discuss the proposition that 'Weber's sociology is a debate with the ghost of Karl Marx.' What does all this amount to?

Nietzsche is the prophet of will, war and power who shuddered at their actualisation in his Germany, made so he believed, coarse and stupid by power and the rise of the masses. Civilisation he argued, was undergoing a *Vermassung*, and consequently a destruction of finesse, critical judgement, creative joy and aristocratic values. Education hastened this process by going over to bourgeois, philistine and military goals of profit, rational efficiency, merely technical and banausic training. Weber, according to Gustav Stolper,* in Munich shortly before his death said in his seminar, 'I have no political plans except to concentrate all my intellectual strength on one problem, how to get once more for Germany a

*G. Stolper, *This Age of Fable*, New York 1942, p. 318n. I give this reference for, if true it deserves record, if untrue, refutation.

great General Staff.' If Weber did actually say this, then I take it as an example of exactly what Nietzsche most deplored. But Nietzsche is never merely single minded, and in this he was like Weber, only with greater strength and in a more extreme position: no one more than Nietzsche warned what the twentieth century could hold of horror and vulgar tyranny; no one more than Nietzche lent the highest powers of mind and expression to ideas on which that tyranny could feed.

To Nietzsche the world had gone wrong through too much Christian virtue; it was corrupted by an excess of charity and mercy, and deceived by the false Christian assertion of an order in things other and better than that which we directly experience. Weber, ambiguous in attitude to his mother's faith and his father's easy materialism, must have found this tempting. We know that Weber's language often caused a scandalous reaction by its brutality and cynicism – something, I suspect, like that '*Potsdamer Ton*' adopted by the servants of the Empire, a tone of speech at once aristocratic and demotic, but always an assault on those to whom it was addressed in its assumption that the world was merely a barrack square. This rejection of the language of human consideration by a man who at other times impressed all who heard him by the beauty of his finely shaped sentences is, I think, a symptom of Nietzchianism at a lower level.

But was Weber greatly influenced by Nietzsche, or did he merely discover in Nietzsche a corroboration of his own divided, unresolved attitudes? I think the latter. Take the questions of 'will' and the 'struggle between values'. Weber, accurately I believe, held that values do not form a single, unambiguous hierarchy, and that no decision, save by consistent individual choice, is possible between competing values. Now of course most people do not bother to try to attain to a consistent position about values. On the contrary they swim in a sea of contradictions, but they can achieve self-direction by the assumption that others will act in ways that can be predicted with probability, and that goals can be attained by rationally calculating and exploiting such probabilities. This type of behaviour is universal: our civilisation in particular has developed it into a dominant mode of conduct and of science. In contrast to this one might set Nietzsche's ethic whereby the superior man – the duty of the inferior is to surrender his will to that of the superior man; a dangerous counsel – shall choose, resolve and act at hazard, gambling with death.

Now Weber does posit an opposite ethic to that of the rational calculation of probabilities and a daily ethic of compromise. It is not, however, Nietzsche's in that it contains variety. Nietzsche's superior man chooses and maintains his choice in terms of the 'will to power' whereas Weber recognises as socially given a whole range of such choices, of such willed life-styles. Those committed to the life of aesthetic or religious values, who pursue honour or abstract duty, are careless of consequences in their commitment, but they have chosen and to attain their ends of virtue they behave rationally enough. Their behaviour is 'value-rational' (*wertrational*) as opposed to a purposeful, judicious rationality (*Zweckrationales Handeln*). Thus Weber is in agreement with Niezsche's attitudes of contempt, but not with Nietzsche's affirmation; that affirmation is but one path, and Weber's pluralism allows him a typical ambiguity.

It may not seem very positive or striking in our time to say that values are not in harmony with each other, that the true may be ugly, the holy repulsive, the beautiful feigning and the good terrible. But in the nineteenth century, even in intellectual circles it was moderately shocking; and to the traditions and faiths of his mother and his wife it was revolutionary and alienating – an explanation, possibly, of the hagiographic falsification which his wife employed in her biography of Weber. To find that science could neither order nor guarantee values was also surprising to both positivists and idealists. Nietzsche and Weber represent a reaction against those assumptions, a reaction, however, that would have seemed in its defiant tone a little excessive to sophisticated Britons who had read their Hume or Frenchmen who had read their Baudelaire. It might also have seemed excessive to men less sheltered than Weber from the everyday deprivations and perils of life outside his privileged world.

The master of that underprivileged world, so his followers claimed, was Karl Marx. In the 1970s when at least a quarter of the world's population lives under regimes which are formerly Marxist, and when to criticise Marxism in the countries of Western Europe and North America is often taken as a proof of ignorance, paranoia or corruption, it is important to remember three things about Weber's age. Marxism was not then a politically dominant creed. Neither was social thought, left and right, permeated by Marxist assumptions, nor was political thought shaped by its present polarities. Nor was the Marx known to that age the Marx of the later twentieth century, either in the vulgar image of Marx as prophet, legislator, and the Newton of the social sciences, or in the polymorphous perverse figure, the infinitely slippery trickster of the mind who only seriously became an object of intellectual consciousness in the 1950s. Weber knew not Stalin, Mao nor Fidel; he did know the young Lukàcs, but the Lukàcs who sat at Weber's feet was caught up in the conflict of values, the concepts of virtue, beauty, and a romantic Slavophilism which reminds one of Rilke's claim that, 'Russia is a country bounded by God'. He was concerned with Tolstoy, Prince Mishkin, Alyosha, rather than with Hegel and the young Marx.

And Weber also knew something of the unfinished story of German Social Democracy.

The real founder of the German Social Democratic Party was Ferdinand Lassalle, but its ideology was formally Marxist. This involved certain practical difficulties. For more than thirty years Marx was a testy middle-aged gentleman – the noun is used accurately – in London. Lassalle was on the whole rather a fine figure, realistic but not base in his politics, romantic in his life. But his party was saddled with Marxism. This involved a belief in apocalyptic revolution, a year greater than '93 in which the despised and rejected of the earth would revenge their ancient wrongs and establish the realm of distributive justice for ever in society. The very condition of '*les damnées de la terre*', as the International has it, was the pledge and the instrument of their triumph. Science and Marxism were identical: by science, historical and economic, it was demonstrated that the future lay with the proletariat. God did not reign in heaven and religion at best was the cry of the heartless world, at worst the opium of the people. But history had replaced God, and history, too, was prophecy; after the judgement of the revolution would come a new heaven and a new earth. And it was the working class, ever exploited, ever in struggle, that was the chariot of history advancing through industrialisation, through the brutalities of economic exploitation, through the recurrent miseries of capitalist crisis to the goal of a just society.

All this was the formal belief system of steelworkers in the Ruhr, miners in Silesia, weavers, shoemakers and worthy men like Bebel in his prison cell taking advantage of the enforced leisure to read science, philosophy and economics. They had wives and families and small savings. They showed great organisational talents and built up a trade union movement. They survived the persecutions – perhaps even thrived on them – of Bismarck's anti-socialist laws which Weber half approved. They took advantage of Bismarck's social legislation which in the early 1880s put Germany ahead of the world in terms of industrial and social assurance. They built up the first mass party on the European continent, a party inevitably bureaucratic, machine-committed and elite-ridden, but theirs. They were also the enduring soldiers of the Empire. When that Empire fell in military disaster on the Western Front their leaders, simple men enough, despised by intellectuals like Weber, found themselves confronting a reality before which their decency, their party cunning, their deference and their ideology were all inadequate. It was through this party of Bebel and Kantsky that Weber perceived, as in a glass darkly, the figure of Marx. The contradiction between the Social Democratic ideology, built on the dream of the apocalyptic revolution, and the Lassallean idea of the permeation and capture of the state by the processes of representative government, became fully evident only in Weber's last years.

In his inaugural lecture at Freiburg in 1895 Weber declared that the workers were politically immature, and incapable of effective power, even though they were certainly right in many of their aims and some of their claims – those recognised by the Evangelical Social Union. At any rate the imperial state was stronger than the Social Democratic Party and, even if that party triumphed, it would become the prisoner of the state and at the same time by its insistence on planning extend the realm of an over-mighty bureaucracy. In 1918, indeed, Weber said his position was hardly to be distinguished from that of the Socialists, but when he accompanied the German delegates to receive the peace conditions laid down in Versailles he spoke of their new masters to Field-Marshal Ludendorff in other terms: 'Do you credit that I take this swinish state of affairs that we now have as democracy?'

Against this background we can, I think, better understand the postures in which Weber confronted Marx. He said of his most famous essay, *The Protestant Ethic and the Spirit of Capitalism*, that it was a factual refutation of the materialist conception of history. (This was published in 1904–5, two years after the first version of a now neglected book, W. Sombart's, *Der moderne Kapitalismus*, to which we shall return.) On a first reading *The Protestant Ethic* is unambiguous: the movement to a capitalist society was primarily caused by the habits, attitudes and beliefs of Protestantism, more specifically of Calvinism, most specifically of English Puritanism. Puritans worked hard in their callings and amassed treasures which the asceticism of their creed did not permit them to consume. Yet that creed did not allow them to let their treasure lie idle. As a result they invested, denied the flesh, and produced a new economic order. But this is not an 'idealist' position, asserting that the world is what men's thoughts make of it, but a claim that ideas as well as economic motives are interests too. As Weber said in another famous essay, *The Social Psychology of the World Religions*, 'Not ideas, but ideals *and* material interests, directly govern men's concepts.' (My italics.) Professor R. Bendix, perhaps the most learned of all commentators on Weber, goes further, correctly I believe, and says, 'according to Weber, material without ideal interests are empty, but ideals without material interests are impotent'. Despite Bendix's accuracy, Weber's position for all his reservations is essentially biased to the 'ideal' position: ideas in their presence or through absence are the main determinants of the social.

Indeed a sound Weberian might say that the above is too strong, for Weber's formal position differs I think from the overall impression made by his work. That formal position is that, first, we are concerned in social studies only to grasp individual action, although of course, such actions have unintended social consequences. Second, Weber holds that any basically uni-casual explanation of all events in society must be false – this is in accord with the neo-Kantian teaching of Rickert which he adopted and Weber's view that the historical sciences, including sociology, are essentially concerned with what is individually specific. It follows from this that while Marx, as a teacher, an undeniably great economic historian and brilliant political analyst, is someone to be learned from, yet he has to be learned from piecemeal, serving as a source of particular illuminations and valuable models to aid one's thinking about the social and historical worlds. But the formal Weber is not the only Weber: to repeat, the real Weber gives to men's concepts and values a paramount role in the drama of social life.

Furthermore, for Weber Marx is imprecise as to what is and is not part of the economic realm. Economic behaviour to Weber, is behaviour which is intended to acquire resources which are also desired by others by means which exclude force and fraud. But non-economic factors affect what is or is not defined as a 'resource' in a specific situation – for example, religious or magical appraisals of what is valuable. Again, purely economic factors can act as the parameters within which non-economic behaviour is possible: the economy itself is a limiting, though not determining, influence on society. Marx's simple economic materialism, Weber believes, dissolves under such considerations. Nor does Marx's lumping of technics into 'the means of production' satisfy him: Weber is surely correct in believing that with any state of technology many economic orders are possible; with any economic order many technologies are compatible.

It is this that leads to a real insight: that there is a problem as to why it was specifically Western Europe that uniquely created industrial capitalism with its still unmeasured consequences as a new kind of society. Marx in a sense gives an answer to this in the first volume of *Capital*, finding it largely but not exclusively in the unique dynamics of the English agrarian system in the age of the Tudors. But Marx does not ask the negative queston, why not elsewhere? Why not China, Rome, India or Peru? Weber does attempt this and he gives an unambiguous reply. This is in truth not to debate with the ghost of Marx, but it is to be more perceptive in a matter of importance not only for historians and sociologists but also for those who, however rashly, would transform contemporary peasants into industrial workers in an industrial milieu.

We may think that the debate between Marx and Weber never really took place. We may hold, too, that we know today, as Weber could not, a new Marx, revealed by scholarship and the publication of suppressed or forgotten manuscripts. Whether this new Marx is superior to the old is, however, another question, for Marx may well have known exactly what he was about when he discarded or withheld so much of his work from publication. In the same way I would suggest that Weber's position in relation to Nietzsche is less interesting than is sometime claimed. Doubtless in his later years Weber found a new strength to express his feelings and attitudes through his reading of Nietzsche and his entry into circles in which Nietzsche's ideas were operative. But Weber did not derive his attitude to the will, to values, or to aristocratic principles from Nietzsche; rather he found corroboration for some of his positions in what he took to be Nietzsche's judgement on the world.

For Weber, Marx was a quarry of ideas and of facts. This aspect of Marx – which by its piecemeal nature is remote from Marxism as theory or ideology – is often neglected. Marx was learned, ingenious, fertile of specific hypotheses and as artful as a wagon-load of monkeys. Weber's debt here is not one of generalised judgement but it is considerable. So also is his obligation to his contemporary Werner Sombart whose learning and ingenuity about the nature of capitalist activity and its sources in war, luxury and group psychology are today undervalued for reasons which derive less from Sombart's real defects than from the subsequent course of German history. (Weber's influence on Sombart was very great, but another story.) But it is the Marx of ideology, prophecy and German social democracy who counts as a major object of Weber's public political consciousness.

7 The Formal Sociology

Although Nietzsche and Marx in their different ways were men concerned to judge and condemn, this did not prevent either from contributing to scholarship both directly and through their influence. Nietzsche's *Birth of Tragedy* may be as completely rejected by orthodox classicists as is the labour theory of value by non-Marxist economists. But classics all the same is intellectually different and richer because of Nietzsche, and our understanding of society and history is the starker for the famous study of the wage worker's day and the attempt to trace the story of capitalist farming in England in the first volume of *Capital*. But though this, and more, is true enough, what characterised these two men was their passionate judgement and their apocalyptic myth.

Now Weber, though a great maker of social mythology, was primarily a scholar. He was a learned man, a researcher, a theorist, seeking to diagnose rather than engage in prophetic judgement. Weber's effort was to attain to a diagnosis not a prognosis of his society, his time and his country. All of his sociology, even when it roams most widely, is concerned with this goal of understanding as completely and clinically as possible.

What can we understand? We can understand the actions of other men – not precisely perhaps, not always certainly, and we can be deceived. Nevertheless, human action is in some measure open to us if only because we, too, are human. This is the first step of Weber's sociology. The second is the identifying of the basic unit of the social – what Weber himself calls the 'atom', a word which I think carried for him not the contemporary un-

derstanding of atoms as complexes of more fundamental
particles which are oddly probabilistic, but an idea of
ultimate irreducibility, of a tiny impenetrable essence.
This atomic unit of the social is the single deliberate
action of an individual directed to affecting the behaviour of one or more persons. Such actions are to be
distinguished from merely idle, automatic or self-directed
deeds by virtue of their having 'intentional reference'.
That phrase means merely what we have already said:
they are performed with the intention of altering the
behaviour of others. The intention is their essence, and
their success, failure, partial success or unintended results are secondary factors. Society is the sum of unit
social acts, but clearly society is not a chaos. These
acts fall into categories and can be combined into structures. It is to Weber the task of his kind of sociology
– he recognises that it is not the only kind – to understand the categories and structures of social actions in
their actual and historical manifestations.

As we have said, Weber's starting point is his conception of the social sciences as *historical* sciences. He is an
historicist in the sense that to him all human reality is to
be understood in the dimension of time and by the
methods of the historian.* Gradually Weber's sociology
emancipates itself from history, but he is always an
historicist, to whom all the categories and structures of
social action are relatively impermanent even when, like
the imperial Chinese bureaucracy which so fascinated
him, they endured for two millennia. He always, so far as
the logic of science and history is concerned, declared
himself a disciple of Heinrich Rickert to whom history
was knowledge of what is unique, specific and individual,
as opposed to the knowledge afforded by the physical
sciences, which was abstract, general and capable of

*The word 'historicism' has other, more recent meanings, but
as an account of Weber this older usage is sufficient.

being stated in the form of invariable natural laws. Out of the chaos of past transactions we select for the purposes of history and the *human* sciences those which relate to human values.

The totality of real events, physical as well as historical, is not to be encapsulated by any science. We can never know with complete knowledge, for the world is too rich. Our systems of laws are not nature's but our own, and are provisional; the task of making and amending them is never done. Sociology complements but does not transcend history in its attempt to grasp the structure of social behaviour, nor can it replace the historian's concern with unique events and persons.

In his historical studies Rickert gave to human values a central place. Outside the stream of temporal events, historians had stood, he claimed, confident in their objectivity, in that the value of truth provides at least one undoubted shared value. Rickert also held that even if all values other than truth are in doubt, no one can dispute that life and history present men with universal and problematic meanings and values. But in these argument Weber tacitly went another way. This, I think, took him far from Rickert. For, as we saw, Weber found values manifest in conflict, and irreducible to a transcendent order. He starts from his own valuations, or from the value-questions of his age. This is a form of relativism, but it is a relativism which is not complete, not without at least one rule. To Weber all history and every sociology is relative, but necessarily and properly so: the realm of values does not guarantee objectivity, but, having chosen his interest and thus asserted his value-position, the historian or sociologist is committed to such objectivity and truth as can, painfully, be attained. Every diagnosis involves, after all, standards and value-judgements, as to the proper working of the patient.

Weber's patient is society. His principal diagnostic

device is the 'ideal type'. An enormous volume of ink has been used in discussing what Weber really meant by this term. My own view is that the problem is both very difficult but also, for any present-day sociology, quite trivial, and that just as one may be bemused by complex legerdemain and yet not seriously occupied by it, so one may regard the whole issue of 'ideal types'. But two things must be said to clear away understandable and recurrent errors. Weber did not mean that his ideal types were in some sense good or noble: 'ideal' here simply means 'not actually exemplified in reality'. No element of value is involved. Secondly, he did not intend his 'ideal typical method' to invent any novel instrument of analysis. Rather, by this he meant to explain and refine what social scientists and historians actually do. The ideal type begins with making overt the tacit, actual methodology of other men, and by making this methodology publicly clear Weber hoped to improve the self-consciousness and rigour of the social sciences.

Why 'ideal'? Plenty of things and people are typical: remarks like, 'He is a typical stockholder', 'That is a typical cardiac lesion', 'There is a typical Picasso', refer to a representative normality of experience. One might if one wished call such examples 'real types'. They can be social: 'That is a typical contract', or 'They have a typical marriage'. But as we said, 'ideal' in Weber's concept means 'not actually exemplified in reality'. So the ideal type is not an extreme 'real type'. If I say, 'He is a typical stockbroker, indeed he is the stockbroker *in excelsis*', then I am still talking about actual things, if of extreme cases. This gets one a little closer to the ideal type, but not all the way. 'Paganini is the perfect violinist', is an extreme case: he has all the qualities of a violinist, *and* I am claiming he has them to perfection. If I mean that perfectly seriously, then, so far as violin-playing is concerned, ideal and reality coincide. But of course they never do: I can always imagine some possible extension of skill or expression that would make Paganini even better. It is this imagination that is the key: the ideal type is the pure case, never actualised, uncluttered by extraneous attributes and ambiguities.

In one way my example of Paganini is misleading in that it makes one think by association of an ideal perfection and excellence. It must be remembered that for Weber there is an ideal type of an embezzlement, of any crime, horror or sin. When one uses such concepts as 'capitalist', 'feudal', 'entrepreneur', 'romantic', 'charismatic' and so on, one is, consciously or not, using ideal types. All such complex descriptive and generalising terms are ideal types in the social sciences.

But why are they not more, why are they not specifications of social reality? Here one comes back to the slipperiness of Weber, his delight, as I think, in the appearance of never being finally committed, but of always having the ace of ambiguity up his sleeve. (It is one part of what the great historian Meinecke meant when he called Weber 'the German Machiavelli.) But this slipperiness is not merely an attitude, but is part of Weber's appraisal of the even greater slipperiness of social reality and of how the Proteus of history may be seized. Society to Weber, as we saw, is made up of the interplay of unit social acts so numerous, so kaleidoscopic that we can only seize and hold them in the mind by some device such as the ideal type, knowing all the time that the device is itself merely a tool, something we have made, not something we have found as a constituent of the real. To be reminded of this is very useful and often salutary, but that is all.

If I sit down to work out a model – as I would call it – of a bureaucratic order, made up of certain elements of hierarchical organisation, specialisation of function, concentration of responsibility, rules of procedure, and so on, I do not say to myself that I am constructing (or analysing) an ideal type. I know perfectly well what I am about, just as M. Jourdain in Molière's *Le Bourgeois gentilhomme* knew exactly what he was saying, even though he was struck with wonder at being told he was speaking prose. The parallel is close : for the purposes of language-study it is important to be able to at least tell most prose from most verse, but it is not of importance to a native-speaker ordering his supper to be distracted by reflection on the fact that he is not doing so in iambics. Methodology is, similarly, a distraction to science except under certain rare circumstances. (Which does not mean that methodology is not worthwhile in itself, to methodologists.) But what of these 'rare circumstances'? I do not mean by them the common scholarly activity of breaking up and re-formulating someone else's system : that is one of the core activities of the knowledge industry. What I do mean is that in principle one can come up against instances where a model or a system of thought can no longer be saved for scientific respectability by any of the devices such as elaboration, the addition of a special theory, etc., which are commonly employed. Such cases have, I believe, occurred in physics during the last century. I can find no evidence of them in the history of the social sciences, but in principle they are possible and even, I would guess, probable. Then we may want to use Weber's full battery of devices and employ all his ambiguous ingenuity. Otherwise we may rest with our rough, in part always unexamined, models of social behaviour.

Weber's great, unfinished, posthumously published book, *Economy and Society* (*Wirschaft und Gesellschaft*), begins as though everything in sociology had to be created *de novo*, out of chaos. This exercise of definition and analysis is complex, powerful, daunting and often exemplary. But of course Weber knew very well that the subjects with which he was concerned had a long genealogy and he accepted much of the vocabulary of previous scholars and his contemporaries – even of those contemporaries with whom he most disputed. His lexicon of concepts consisted of items taken from law, history, economics and philosophy. This lexicon provided the foundations of his attempt to reconstruct society, even if not into a single comprehensible scientific model, by advancing a number of models which would enable society, as it concerned and interested him, to be diagnosed. This meant that Weber had to have some kind of working classification of the various major forms of social action. One way to that classification would have been by the kind of institutional study carried out by his exact English contemporary, Leonard Hobhouse. But this was not Weber's way. With Hobhouse he shared a concern with rationality, but Weber was to attack directly, not by way of institutions. He attempted to classify all acts under four heads, complexly related.

An act, to Weber, is rational when it can be described as being in accord with the canons of logic, the procedures of science or of successful economic behaviour; that is to say, when it is end-attaining in its intentions and in full accord with factual knowledge and theoretical understanding in its means. Where the choice of an end from among other ends and the choice of means satisfies these criteria an act is fully rational. On the other hand, where the ends are given by values – religious, moral or aesthetic – or where such values affect the choice of means then we have behaviour classified as 'value-rational'. However, if the ends of an act are accepted for reasons of tradition – a kind of value – and the means, which need not thereby be ineffective, are given also by tradition in whole or part, we have behaviour of a kind which has been the dominant mode in most societies of most ages. Finally, according to Weber, acts may be merely moved by the affections and passions – 'affectual action'. This kind of behaviour is, when the end and the means are both derived from the emotions, at the opposite pole in Weber's system from the calculatingly rational deed.

Now Weber is not completely consistent throughout his work in his use of these categories. What is more, if we use ends and means as sub-categories of behaviour a wide variety of forms – at least ten – of behaviours is comprehended. How are these empty, classificatory boxes to be filled? And where does the concept of 'charisma' which we met at the outset fit in? To answer these points we will have to become more concrete; but before that we must look at another set of Weber's categories, a set which is concerned with the central practical interests, public and private, of his life. What is the basis of political obligation, of our uncoerced obedience to the state? Traditionally this is the central problem of British and French political philosophy. In imperial Germany the question could be answered, given that history of varied elements and that constitution of heterogeneous claims and institutions, by many routes. Not one of these was clearly adequate. For what constitutes the *legitimacy* of power? To what secular authority should a man bow? Weber argues that power which is regarded as legitimate by the obedient ceases to be naked power or coercion, and becomes authority by three paths: these are the traditional, the rational-legal and the charismatic.

According to the traditional path time makes good; we have always done things in such a way and obeyed people of such a family or holders of such an office who have got into the office by a recognised quality of holiness or valour or merit: these are the forms of traditional authority. There is a wisdom in old things and the *mos maiorum*. But why should time legitimate? It is not obvious, and I believe that it is thought to do so only where the past is felt to have at one time been sacred, being endowed with a holy quality that can be explained by reference to the actions of the gods, or an accord with a partially or wholly lost age of virtue or a semi-divine establishment of families or institutions. Both those who command and those who obey must accept these beliefs and feelings.

As regards the rational-legal path, reason is being; reason is science, is technical, is law : these are the foundations of rational-legal authority. In this case the legitimacy is that of a unique efficiency. Rational-legal authority is supremely good at the attainment of ends. I believe that here too there is much of the sacred although in a special form; for there does exist the faith in certain industrial societies that science, and scientific procedures, and procedures that mimic what are believed to be the forms of science, are imbued with the idea of the holy. This is not, of course, the whole story – though such a faith was very typical of the Hohenzollern empire in the heroic age of German science and industrialisation, just as it is prevalent today, especially in Communist countries. However that may be, Weber is not concerned with this possibility. The legal-rational is, to him, what it claims to be : what he questions and deplores are its consequences.

According to Weber's final argument divine grace is self-guaranteeing, and disobedience to it is blasphemy; here is the claim of the charismatic leader or prophet : God cannot be other than the ultimate legitimacy. (For God, where necessary, read *the class*, *the people*, *the folk, the march of history, inevitable destiny*, and so on : secular idolatry is still the worship of images.) Charisma is neither long-enduring nor extensible very far. Those who accept the charismatic authority of their leader do so as a chosen band. The demands of everyday life for order, continuity and predictability, cannot be reconciled with a constant eruption of divine inspiration. Charisma, then, becomes routinised in ritual, administration and discipline.

Coercive power seeks legitimacy for itself, and even those who are coerced by it tend to try to find some legitimacy in their fate and thus in their rulers. There is a quest to accept, to find or invent legitimacy as part of a general quest which Weber seems to think a universal human characteristic. Human life seeks meaning: society is made possible, however precariously, by meaning and value or that search for them which is itself an embodiment of meaning – since no quest can be undertaken without a conviction, however doubting, that the intention and the goal are worthwhile.

Thus in a sense Weber's end is his beginning. We are back with the unavoidability of valuation, of choice where there is incompatibility and contradiction and no transcendent order. The world of man in society is a world of unit social acts, ordered by the need to make choices for an always uncertain future in terms of some principle of choice which we call a value. It has been objected that existence and value-choice cannot be conceptually separated from each other: I do not see that this is a criticism of Weber, but rather an affirmation of his position.

Weber the sociologist was indeed an existentialist *avant la lettre*. This claim has little to do with Weber's relationship to Nietzsche and nothing to do with his encounter with Kierkegaard under the influence of young Lukács. Nevertheless, I think the term 'existentialist' is precisely accurate as a description of what lies at the heart of Weber's theory of society.

But if that is so, Weber in his personal life and in his deployment of his sociology as an expression of his own being is a very odd existentialist. Again and again we find him resisting commitment and engagement and welcoming ambiguity or indecision. Yet even then he goes no further, undertaking neither the Pyrrhonism nor the poetic insight into the metaphorical nature of all discourse which are the justifications of irony. Thus he was, I suppose, an existentialist constantly guilty of bad faith. Some, of course, would call his form of 'bad faith' scientific integrity.

It is certainly very human. Weber practised at least one part of what he preached. This world of ours is, just because it is human, in principle open to human understanding. We are not limited, as with nature, to a search for laws, but we can – making use of such sociological 'laws' as we can discover – hope to go further and know the causal and motivational nexus which yields a specific social situation. Such a situation may well be a very foreign one from a remote culture, but it cannot but be humanly accessible. Thus tacitly Weber accepts a psychic unity of humankind. Weber's strongest claim to sociological greatness, I suppose, comes here in that, alone of the greatest sociologists of his age, he faced the fullness of history and attempted to bring to it human sympathy and humane imagination to serve as the foundations of sociological method. Of course in his actual practice he was limited by his own human capacities.

8   The Substantive Sociology

Society is problematic because we cannot foreknow all the consequences – nor for that matter all the determinants – of our acts. Act as we may with a maximum of calculated rationality, based on a careful assessment of empirically tested evidence, we still act with others, and the results of our deeds, even if we attain our purposes, are not exhausted by our goals. No one sat down in the centuries that followed the decline of the Carolingine empire and decided to establish that order which we call feudalism, first in Northern France, thereafter in England, Sicily, the Latin Kingdom of Jerusalem and elsewhere. Rather that regime emerged out of the desire for power and the need for order, the tenacity of possession and the obedience of prudence, of innumerable people. No one intends to establish a market economy : such a state of affairs comes into being through the individual bargaining arrangements of people exchanging goods or services to maximise their advantages or minimise their deprivations. And so on : the Anglo-Dutchman Mandeville saw how 'private vices' by their demands on the economy could prove to be 'public benefits'. To that most perfect social scientist Adam Smith the allocation of resources that results from the interactions of the market produced a result in concordance with what would be the fiat of a supremely calculating force of reason. But there was no such force. It was as though some 'invisible hand' was at work, the god-like hand of an omnipotent accountant. In Germany, Kurt called such enormous unintended consequences the 'heteronomy of ends'. We work more than we can mean or know.

Feudalism and the capitalism of a free market economy are ideal types. Even in the England of William the Conqueror or the Antioch of Bohemond feudalism as a model was not perfectly exemplified. Even in England between 1846 and 1871 a free market capitalist economy was not to be found of the type that economists described and, increasingly, prescribed. (Neither was the case stronger in late-nineteenth century America with its state intervention to aid those who grasped for economic power, nor in imperial Germany, where the state was a part of the economic order, intervening both in the labour market in the interests of domestic harmony, and also in the pattern of finance and industry in the interests of national might.) Now Weber would certainly have disapproved of the phrase I am going to use, for it commits sins against the merely heuristic intent which he professed and against his nominalism; but I believe it accurately describes what his substantive work is concerned to do: that concern was to put flesh on the bony skeleton of the ideal types, choosing those particular ideal types which demonstrate the trickster quality in society, that is, which are abstractions of phenomena exemplifying the heteronomy of ends.

In his early, enormously detailed studies of the conditions of the rural workers east of the Elbe – studies essentially without an upshot, although directed to questions of practical policy – Weber is dealing with the consequences of economic rationality. Semi-servile statuses for the workers involve also social obligations for the masters. In the east of the Empire where the expansion of the Teutonic Knights, the Electors of Brandenberg and Frederick the Great had resulted in Junker rule over a partly alien, Polish-speaking and Catholic, under-class, economic rationality – i.e., the desire to maximise profits – was wakening the German nature of the region. Immigrant Slavs were coming into a society always in part colonial. They were a rural proletariat, whose only social relations with the rulers were economic. The bonds of servility and obligation no longer held. Workers in principle might become tenant farmers, but they were psychologically 'proletarianised'. They demanded more cash. They could not compete economically with the culturally inferior Slavs * – yet it was to the cash interest of landlords to employ these Slavs. The Junkers, the heart of Prussian power, fiercely loyal in politics, were yet in the economic sphere a menace to the security of the eastern marches. The Slavs were not just a threat to patriarchal relations and old solidarities but also a symptom of the clash between an old Germany and a new, between the interests of the economy and the maintenance of Germany as a 'power state'. And none of this had been consciously willed.

Weber is *par excellence* the sociologist of the economic order. He does not confuse economics with sociology, but he believes that the sociologist must be concerned with purely economic institutions, such as stock markets, just because they are institutions and are thus societal objects. Also the sociologist has to be aware that major social formations – paramountly those of religion and of the family – have economic consequences. These consequences are in turn limiting factors – even at times determinants – of the social situation. Economic resources and economic arrangements condition social interests. But the resulting sociology of the economic order is elab-

---

*Weber was not a racialist. He believed, however, in an inherent superiority in Germany which can be called cultural at best, mystical at worst. In his latter years certain Russians such as Tolstoy and Soloviev came to mean much to him intellectually. But he never seems to have really considered Poles or Russians at large as good as his fellow-countrymen – as peoples with equal rights to their own inspirations or with equal, if different, virtues and qualities.

orate, confusing and confused. If Weber had lived he might have refined it, but I doubt this. The elaboration and muddle are as present in the early studies of the rural workers in the east as they are painstakingly made manifest in the incomplete, posthumous *Economy and Society*.

What Weber is trying to do is nothing less than to comprehend capitalism as a civilisation, the civilisation of the modern western world. To him capitalistic activity is all but a universal feature of human societies. Viking raiders and the priestly treasurers of archaic divine kingdoms, for example, are engaged in capitalistic action. But capitalism itself is historically extremely concrete. To understand even the petty issues of farming in eastern Germany one must understand the uniqueness of capitalism as a western system, historically specific. In the lectures published after his death as *General Economic History* Weber gives a formal specification of capitalism : it is present 'wherever the industrial provision for the needs of a human group is carried out by the methods of enterprise, irrespective of what [particular] need is involved. More specifically, a rational capitalistic establishment is one with capital accounting, that is, an establishment which determines its income yielding power by calculation according to the methods of modern bookkeeping and the striking of a balance.'

Capitalism then is not merely western but comparatively modern. Weber ascribes the accountant's balance sheet to the Dutchman Stevin – and in my edition of Weber gets Stevin's dates a century late – but in fact double-entry accounting and the balance-sheet are pre-Reformation Italian devices. But Weber does give the recent fact of capitalism very ancient origins in western society. The tendency to an increasing component of rational action in society as against traditional modes begins in ancient Greece, and the invention of coined money by the Greeks is an illustration of this fact, for money makes quantitative economic rationality easily possible as a common measure both of things and of abstractions such as 'work' and 'risk'. Disciplined armies are highly rational means to ends; so is religious discipline which at its peak in western monasticism orders men to their eternal goal. To Weber there is in all rationality a component of deprivation: the soldier is deprived of his spontaneous and reflecting being – the Prussian army was based on a complete automatism of ordered obedience which Weber both approved and deplored – and the monk too is not just ascetic – that is true of all hermits and of the monasticism of the Thebaid – but a disciplined ascetic. Disciplined deprivation is in Weber's thought an essential aspect of rational action in the pursuit of its ends. The capitalist is the ascetic of economic gain. Capitalism is the manifestation of a spirit, a character: it is much more than a constellation of productive, exchange and accounting devices.

It is worth remarking at this point that Weber is really very little interested in industrialism as such. In his treatment of the transformation of technology and organisation which we call the industrial revolution, the factory and factory labour, the enormous and continuing transformation of productivity which distinguishes industrial societies from all previously existing modes of life and society, Weber is merely conventional and often cursory. Despite this commentators have tried to make much of him as an industrial sociologist – we saw earlier his empirical interest in the attitudes and experiences of industrial labour – but it is impossible to see Weber as a major analyst in this area. His contemporaries Werner Sombart, J. A. Hobson and Thorstein Veblen in Germany, England and America are rich – particularly the latter two – where Weber is poor. It is this point, I think, that also renders so many of the comparisons of Marx with Weber pointless. Their concerns are too often not the same. Criticism of Marx, an instructive pursuit, is only in one sense valuably conducted by comparison with Weber, and that sense has nothing to do with the sociology of the industrial order.

But if we say that capitalism is its spirit, what do we mean? Capitalism to Weber is a huge historical movement in a specific geographical and cultural area, so polymorphous and perverse in its course and origins that all generalisations must fall unusually short of the reality. Thus we must weave a net in which to fish up this leviathan out of many inter-linked ideal types, and we must use that net with caution and after long practice at the trawl. One can regard Weber's life as that practice and *Economy and Society* as the net. The use of the term 'spirit' is then cautionary: its very vagueness is necessary where all is so tentative.

The above paragraph, I think, represents Weber and the pieties about this part of his work adequately, but it also does him less than justice in that he was too good a scholar and thinker to be always consistent. I am quite clear that he thought capitalism was the consequence of the actions of a limited number of men who possessed (or were possessed by) a common spirit which produced a complex of rational modes of profit-making – which complex is what we call 'capitalism'. With Weber we are to view this spirit and its unintended consequences from the top downwards: capitalism is the work of capitalists, not the common experience of a special kind of society. Weber was to claim that he was not trying to explain the origin of capitalism by this spirit of the capitalists, but I don't think one can read him and also accept this recurrent point, typical of his ambiguously polemical style.

Posterity has not been wrong in its concentration on the long essay, or series of fragments, published in 1904–5 as *The Protestant Ethic and the Spirit of Capitalism*. It is extraordinarily interesting and it carries with it the conviction, justly, that somewhere in the area of its concerns lies an important but not fully formed truth about society. To have read it is necessary for any understanding of our age. Weber starts off from the commonplace position of his time that Protestantism is correlated with predominant wealth and power in the form we know as capitalism. Is this accidental? We have seen that there were capitalistic activities before capitalism and in non-capitalist societies. There were also capitalists before the Reformation, but Weber disposes of them cavalierly enough as exceptional 'supermen of economic rationality'. But capitalism and the Reformation as major historical movements are too closely linked in time for any mere contingent play of events to be a probable account of what happened. Indeed, an examination of how theological positions, everyday ethics and economic behaviour run together forces us to conclude that there does exist some causality.

The theology on which Weber concentrates is Calvinism. But Calvin and Knox were not concerned to change traditional economic ethics and their views triumphed both in areas like Holland where capitalism was early manifest and in Scotland and Geneva where it developed fairly late. Even so, Weber extends the working of Calvinism to English and colonial American Puritanism and then to other forms of Protestantism. How just this extension, vital to Weber's case, may be we cannot pursue here. However, in Calvinism one has no confidence of election to salvation: all one can do is to have faith and re-inforce that faith by diligent, self-denying labour in one's vocation. One can never relax, and unremitting strenuous work at one's trade and in life, prayer and worship are obligatory. (One can in fact find little basis for all this in Calvin's *Institutes* and contrary counsel in Knox, but I think Weber is correct enough in his picture of how Calvinism actually understood.) Toil to Puritan preachers expelled evil, impure, pleasure-seeking and sensual impulses. Time, God's greatest, briefest gift, must not be wasted. The fruits of toil might signify divine approval, if they were not enjoyed. As an everyday ethic, Weber argues, this theology led to the accumulation of capital. Its unintended consequence was capitalist society. Finally, the ethic could be and was separated from the theology and became an autonomous secular force, 'adequate to modern capitalism in its formative time'.

Weber hedges this account around with reservations. He hints more than he says. He insists that he is showing us only one side of the coin and that the other, the material interests and socio-economic situation of Europe, is also there. But the drift is unmistakeable. In this unique transformation of traditional Europe to capitalism it is what people thought and believed that was decisive. This thesis is borne out in two ways: elsewhere, as for example in his justly famous essay on the sociology of the city and in his lectures on economic history, Weber does turn the coin over. But so far as novel suggestions about the sources of capitalism are concerned he has very little to tell us. Secondly Weber was to write a great deal more about religion in society. One of the core things in these writings is the demonstration that the creeds and establishments of non-European faiths, lacking the drive and burden of anything like a Protestant ethic, did not lead even advanced and complex societies into the rational order of capitalism.

What Weber is concerned with in the sociology of religion is of course not religion in itself, its truth or falsity, nor is it the elaboration of a general theory, like Durkheim's of the function of the religious in the social: it is the working of religion on everyday life, on political, administrative, economic, and moral behaviour in different historical situations that he tries to understand and reduce to order.* The process of understanding means that the sociologist must put himself in a curious position of suspense between a universal scepticism and an equally universal acceptance of thought-worlds other than his own. This suspense is both a source of tension and, to those who enjoy the spectator's ambiguous role, of pleasure. But the task itself is, I think, misconceived: the varieties of religious expression in the banality of common life are too great, too much studied, for an approach that is neither Durkheimian nor Spencerian to succeed.

Primarily there are two alternative religious modes. (It must be remembered that Weber was no ethnologist, even of the armchair.) There are those religions which adapt men to the world, making tolerable by law and ritual the disorder of experience, and the religions of salvation which accept the disorders and perils of being with resignation, repudiate the pleasures of the world, and seek a transcendent otherworldly goal. In his study of Confucianism and Taoism (translated misleadingly under the title *The Religion of China*) Weber finds the best exemplification of a religion that is this-worldly, concerned with the right conduct, that is the ritual conduct, of men here and now, in Confucianism. Ethics are bureaucratised; laws are legitimated by being sacred, but the sacred thing about them is the letter, not the spirit. In fact, emperors and priests might be better served by more personal justice than by such formal laws, but the interest groups on whom they rely press them into this ritual, subtle formalism. Traditional Judaism in the non-prophetic age belongs to the same species as Confucianism, but as the religion of a minority it has a double code – inward and strong, outward and more permissive. In such religions the problematic nature of being

*Hence Weber's sociology of religion is of a piece with all his sociology.

is lost sight of; meaning is devalued, practice elevated. Priests are functional office-holders and teachers of right conduct.

By contrast the religions of salvation turn on issues of meaning; charismatic leaders emerge in them and prophecy is one of their modes. Time does not so much legitimate them but, often by way of tribulation, redeems. It can redeem by works of virtue or of observance – to Weber in this context that means a rejection of rationality – or of participation through ecstasy, mystical or orgiastic, in the other-worldly divine nature. Such faiths have stored in them revolutionary and unpredictable potential.

When in the salvation religions there is present an actual saviour figure, bridging the natural and non-natural gulf, then believers move through society with a confidence at once somnambulistic and frighteningly autonomous. Invariably the relation between salvation religions and their social structures is one of tension, and where salvation is mediated by a redeemer then the tension is maximised: men desert their primordial bonds of kin and place, they question the economic order and its calculating rationality – even Confucianism opposed rational capitalistic behaviour, not because it was in anyway like a creed of salvation, but because its legitimacy was that of tradition – and they call in doubt the political hierarchy because it is a hierarchy and a denial of the brotherhood of the saved in which there are neither bond nor free. Salvation is individual but not local: all men may share, and its values are in principle universal, that is to say, socially unbounded. But, alas, societies *are* their boundaries, both internal and external.

As we saw, the gifts of the spirit become routinised. Compromise, institutionalisation and bureaucracy supervene. Religions become dogmatic and learned, and hence new tensions develop, whereby this learning in its turn comes into conflict with the even more rational-istic learning of the secular order, of philosophy, scholar-ship and positive science. Nor is religious learning a food for the soul hungry for salvation. Routinised and learned, caught in a double bind with the secular order and the demands of faith, charisma and new beginnings inter-vene. The cycle – though Weber does not call it that – resumes in a new form. There is in religion a war and a succession of three ideal types, the magician, the priest and the prophet. More deadly still is the war of all three with the secularised man of learning, suspending belief in the interest of rational understanding. This war Weber does not so much examine as exemplify.

This growth of the rational component of behaviour is to be found too, according to Weber, in the history of law which begins in charisma and religion, separates and secularises out of this origin, and becomes a source of tension for the religions of ritual order and, more strongly, of salvation. Law as lawyer's law, rationally in-strumental, is an index of the growth of secularisation. Together with economic rationality it is the nemesis of an order of meaning in which society is in touch with and bound to the sacred. In such a writer as Kant we find ethical rationality as a prescription in its most extreme and most demanding form, confronting men with duties unmediated by emotion or tradition which, when em-bodied in jurisprudence, imposes a tyranny of reason on the weak and human too great to be endured for long.

Justice in ceasing to be divine becomes necessary. I do not mean by that a practical necessity, but a neces-sity ascribed to things. Reason as sovereign over action justifies all instrumentalities of behaviour and all the con-sequent conditions of men. A rational market economy is in this sense just. Those who are disadvantaged by it are made lowly by necessity in accord with reason. To Weber class – as distinct from Indian castes or the feudal social estates – is a reflection in society of the working of the quantitative rationality of the market. It is manifest by who gets what and who does what in capitalist society: what people get and do does not consist only in income, capital and work, but in 'life chances'. These are the expectations, probabilistically estimable, of length and quality of life. Social status is a function of the general estimation of life chances as good or ill, as invidious or as conferring prestige in the rationality, the highest of all rationalities, of capitalism. There is, however, no reason to expect the lowly to like this: on the contrary one must expect them to struggle above all by instrumental politics against a society thus ordered. But in a world of so many factors and considerations should one wish then to succeed? As we know Weber answered that ambiguously. And can they succeed? I do not believe that Weber thought that they could do more than win by rational political and economic organisation an alleviation of their position.

Thus we are left with one possibility, that of a charismatic politics of the masses making all things new: in what shape of promise or of terror Weber could not tell.

The English sociologist Hobhouse, at much the same time as Weber, worked also with comparable learning on a greater range of data concerning the values and the faiths of men. One of his principles was that there is a secular tendency for the role of reason to increase, despite reversals or divagations, in human affairs. Reason to Hobhouse confronted and comprehended the irrational in action, but was not tainted by it. Reason teased out the constituents of actual situations and the value-problems associated with them. Reason thus resolved conflicts and brought an increasing, if never perfect harmony to human affairs. In many of the specific analyses Hobhouse's *Morals in Evolution* and *Social Development* are superior to what Weber has to say at corresponding points – see, for example, the great chapter on justice and law in the earlier book. Like Weber, Hobhouse flirted with the political and learned from his experiences as a leader writer on the *Manchester Guardian* under C. P. Scott, its most famous editor, and with the trade unions. He had the enormous advantage over Weber of understanding what had been established about the structure and function of social institutions from Ferguson to Spencer. But, unlike Weber, he was not driven by demons and terrors nor sophisticated by being sly and ambiguous. As a result he has left us no diagnosis of his time to reverberate in the minds of men in our later age.

Weber formally evades any scheme of stages of social development or any systems of historical cycles, and yet it is impossible not to find in him both such a scheme and a kind of recurrent cycle. The advantage of rational action is gaining advantage : it is in the business of trying to attain ends, the most effective of the devices produced by the historical experience of mankind. Thus it gradually tends to supplant all other modes of social action. The concept of positive science, deliberate technical innovation, uniform rational social control and law, dispassionate and impersonal administration, and calculated economic action are all historical products characteristic, in their developed forms, of European civilisation. These forms were bought at the price of the deprivations and individual burdens of Protestantism. Where the religious order avoided these specific asceticisms and demands then the most rational of all social systems, advanced capitalism, did not emerge. (To Weber 'rational' is a value-word, although he does not equate 'rational' with 'good'.) There is in all societies a tendency towards an increasing component of rationality in social life, but only in our societies is this movement fully actualised. This tendency involves the displacement from life of the emotional and the traditional modes of legitimate behaviour as socially unacceptable. As a result the world loses its savour. The spontaneous affections of the heart, the hatreds of the moment, the comely and honourable ways of tradition, are all forbidden. Reason illuminates all being with a shadowless and clinical light before which fly poetry, faith and myth. One does not even find in the merciless light of reason the consolation of injustice : reason is its own justification, the legitimator of its own necessities.

Weber took from the poet Schiller a phrase that is usually translated as 'the disenchantment of the world'. The German, in fact, means something more precise : the driving out of magic from things. The magus Weber is the last magician, a Prospero who must bury his staff under the grey sky of everyday rationality. He was himself an unspecialised man : the world of reason is a world in which men lose their manifold natures in the specialised division of labour, devoting themselves to unambiguously defined tasks. Weber's life was a struggle against such a destiny – the destiny of the bureaucrat, the office-holder in big government or big business or big political parties. It is, he wrote, 'the dictatorship of the officials, not of the proletariat, that is marching on'. He did not love this fact.

He found the orderly routine of a secularised world oppressive and calculating, and mechanical order crushing. He loved the power of the state that embodied these things and hated that state for embodying them. He loved that freedom, which he understood as the liberty of the educationally privileged and economically secure, that is, as the precarious product of inegalitarian society in its historical movement. People will always be in tension with the social roles that society requires them to play; and freedom is the rare consequence for a few when that tension accidentally is relaxed. Objectively in a world of rationality, of bureaucracy and the masses one should not expect its survival. Indeed, we should expect disenchantment to become complete, bureaucracy and regulation universal, and secularisation to displace all the meanings of faith and hope while administrative welfare eliminates charity.

But, after all, this scheme of development is itself but another ideal type. And there is in history a lesson of a cyclical kind. When the world is over-routinised, over-bureaucratised, then the prophets and the Caesars return, dowered with charisma. But is that a hope? As I said at the end of the last chapter Weber did not know and he never loved Caesars. His own constitution-mongering in his last days as the Weimar republic came painfully to birth is not very impressive and is caught between an ingenuity about electoral and constitutional arrangements and the wariness of the magus who knows that all his spells will lose their power if he finally commits himself as a participant in the struggles of value in the arena of politics. It is in this diagnosis that the secret of Weber's continued reputation most resides. Like all of him it offers us tension, polarity and ambiguity.

There is, however, another Weber, and that Weber is another matter. The American sociologist Talcot Parsons discovered Weber's work in the 1920s. From it he extracted and elaborated something latent, a systematic sociology of great range and power, although at the moment not very fashionable. This system, carried by Parson's energy and ability far beyond anything that Weber achieved and embodying other constituents from both the larger sociological tradition and from Parson's own researches, is undoubtedly Weberian. It is at once an invention and a discovery. But it is not, I think, all there is in Weber: its very articulation and specificity which are its strengths (and which expose it, therefore, to attack) somehow deny the liquid and evasive richness which is the secret of Weber's strongest sorcery over all his successors.

In his last years Weber, as we saw, moved on the margins of the zone of torrid friendship at the centre of which was the poet Stefan George. In a late poem, 'Man and Satyr', George has the goat-man sneer, 'You are but man ... our wisdom begins where your wisdom ends.' The Man replies that the day of myth is over and the Satyr's time is done. Yet, says the Satyr, 'it is only through magic that life stays awake.' (*Nur durch den Zauber bleibt das Leben wach*) He might not much have liked such teaching, but it is the lesson of Max Weber all the same.

Max Weber left many problems to his readers. His most important book, *Economy and Society*, for example, was edited from disordered, fragmentary manuscripts without even the guidance of a plan or table of the proposed contents. It is now available in English in a complete version, well introduced by G. Roth and published in three volumes (New York, 1968). But should the reader begin there? I think not. He would do better to tackle *Economy and Society* by way of its parts, in *The City* Glencoe, Ill. and London, 1958) or in the quite admirably translated and prefaced volume of essays, *From Max Weber*, edited by Gerth and Mills, (New York and London, 1946) which contains much of the best of *Economy and Society*. If he is very strong, however, the beginner might meet the book head-on with the translation of Part 1 under the title of *The Theory of Social and Economic Organisation* (Edinburgh, 1945) translated by A. M. Henderson and Talcott Parsons. The best preface to that, however, is Parsons' own book, *The Structure of Social Action* (New York, 1937). That important study is, very reasonably, a massive labour in its own right. So, the essays apart, *Economy and Society* is probably not the place to begin.

For the reader who comes to Weber by way of religion the situation is easier. In 1930 Parson's translation of *The Protestant Ethic and the Spirit of Capitalism* (London and New York) was published with an introduction by R. H. Tawney whose own *Religion and the Rise of Capitalism* is still the perfect complement to Weber. A hostile critique, from the enormous controversy on *The*

Protestant Ethic, is K. Samuelsson, *Religion and Economic Action* (London, 1961): more pious orthodoxies will be found in S. M. Eisenstadt, ed., *The Protestant Ethics, and Modernisation: A Comparative View* (New York, 1968). If the reader is less concerned with the Christian tradition decent – not more – translations are *The Religion of China* (1951), *Ancient Judaism* (1952), *The Religion of India* (1958) all published Glencoe, Ill. In the most interesting of these, the study of Confucianism and Taoism, the articles by O. B. van der Sprenkel, 'Chinese Religion', *British Journal of Sociology*, V, 1954 and 'Max Weber on China', *History and Theory*, III, 1961 are necessary correctives. The section of *Economy and Society* on *The Sociology of Religion* appeared separately under that title (Boston and London) in 1964. It is a very barren text. A modern Weberian approach to religion is M. Hill, *A Sociology of Religion* (London, 1973).

Historians may find Weber's *General Economic History* (London, 1927) interesting, although it is untypical. These lectures are, as history, not much, but they do show Weber's mind at work both in its generalising strengths and its weaknesses of structure. More revealing, though it is formally about law and in fact is yet another chunk of *Economy and Society*, is *Max Weber on Law in Economy and Society*, edited by M. Rheinstein (Cambridge, Mass., 1954). A very simple introduction to Weber's historical sociology of law – and all the better for its simplicity – is 'Law, Reason and Sociology' by Clarence Morris (*University of Pennsylvannia Law Review* Vol. 107, 1958). Marxists ought to have a great deal to say that is of importance about Weber and the interpretation of history. On the whole, however, from Bukharin onwards, the Marxists have let us down. Marcuse and Lukàcs are disappointing on Weber. Perhaps some of the Polish Marxist writers are, as is claimed, better, but their books and articles have not been translated. Very useful, in the tradition of historical idealism, is C. Antoni, *From History to Sociology* (London, 1962). The essays on Troeltsch, Meineckse and Weber are particularly recommended.

Methodologists and students of the philosophy of the social sciences are well served. If one believes this an important area then, in addition to Runciman's book cited in the bibliography there are the tough, well-translated three essays which make up *Max Weber on the Methodology of the Social Sciences* (Glencoe, Ill., 1949). The collected papers of one of the translators of these essays on methodology, E. A. Shils, are about to be published by the University of Chicago Press: all his writings on Weber, too numerous to list here, deserve attention in the same way as do those of Talcott Parsons.

There is no full 'life and times' of Weber in English. W. Mommsen's book is specialised and iconoclastic – see bibliography – but should be translated. R. Bendix gives not so much a portrait – see bibliography – as a map, but it is the best map anywhere available of the terrain of Weber's work and makes an excellent supplement and companion to the *From Max Weber* volume. These two are probably, taken together, the irreducible minimum equipment for the English-speaking student of Weber.

Practically all that is written on Weber is written in awe. This may be just, but it does get in the way of understanding: when one is knocking one's forehead on the floor one's vision is certainly limited and probably blurred. It is remarkable that despite this awe so much written about Weber is so good, even if so incomplete. The translations, however, are another matter: they are sometimes, as I have tried to note, good; but often they are stilted, difficult and more obscure than the originals. Nor have all Weber's translators a decent knowledge of English usage. If Weber matters, then much remains to be done both by way of translation and interpretation.

Most of all we need a historical sociology of social thought in early twentieth century Europe such as no writer has yet attempted on a sufficient scale or with sufficient rigour. To say this is not to belittle such a book as Hughes' *Consciousness and Society*, but rather to say that after fifteen years it still stands very much alone. This is a pity for more reasons than the study of Weber, for our century has apparently dedicated itself, only half knowingly, to acting out the ideas and dreams of those years in deadly earnest. All in all the writer who in my opinion comes closest to getting the public Weber right was T. S. Simey in chapters 4 and 5 of his *Social Science and Social Purpose* (London, 1968), but Lord Simey, alas, did not live to develop his approach in depth.

Chronology

1864 Max Weber born at Erfurt, Thuringia on 21 April.
1869 Moves with his family to Berlin.
1879 Confirmed as church member.
1882 Student of economics, philosophy and Roman Law at Heidelberg University.
1883 Military service.
1884 Student at Berlin.
1885 Student at Göttingen.
1889 Completion of his thesis on medieval trading companies.
1891 Qualifies as university teacher with thesis on Roman agrarian and legal history.
1892 Teaches law in Berlin; marries Marianne Schnitzer.
1894 Professor of political economy at Freiberg.
1897 Professor of economics at Heidelberg. 'Nervous breakdown.'
1899–1904 Travels in Europe and (1904) North America.
1903 Made 'Honorarprofessor' – i.e. put in semi-retirement – at Heidelberg.
1904–5 Publication of both parts of *The Protestant Ethic*.
1914–18 Serves in hospital administration.
1918 Professor of sociology at Vienna.
1919 Professor of sociology at Munich.
1920 Dies 14 June.

Bibliography

I THE WRITINGS OF MAX WEBER

1889 *Zur Geschichte der Handelsgesellschaften im Mittelal-
ter.* Stuttgart: F. Enke. (On the history of medieval
trading companies.)

1891 *Die römische Agrargeschichte in ihrer Bedeutung für
das Staats- und Privat-recht.* Stuttgart: F. Enke. (The
agricultural history of Rome in its relation to public
and private law.)

1892 *Die Verhältnisse der Landarbeiter im ostelbischen
Deutschland* (Vol. 55, *Schriften des Vereins für Sozialpolitik*). Berlin: Duncker & Humblot. (The conditions
of rural labour in Germany beyond the Elbe.)

1920–21 *Gesammelte Aufsätze zur Religionssoziologie.* 3
vols, Tübingen: J. C. B. Mohr. (Collected papers on
the sociology of religion.)

1921 *Gesammelte politische Schriften.* Munich: Drei Mas-
ten Verlag. (Collected political writings.)

1924 *Gesammelte Aufsätze zur Soziologie und Sozialpolitik.*
Tübingen: J. C. B. Mohr. (Collected papers on sociology and social policy.)

1924 *Gesammelte Aufsätze zur Sozial- und Wirtschaftsgeschichte.* Tübingen: J. C. B. Mohr. (Collected papers
on social and economic history.)

1924 *Wirtschaftsgeschichte.* Munich: Duncker & Humblot.
(English translation, *General Economic History.* S.
Hellman & M. Palyi, eds. Frank H. Knight, translator.
London: Collier Macmillan, 1961.)
(In subsequent critical editions the pagination of the
original German editions of the posthumous collec-
tions has been maintained.)

2 SOME BOOKS ON WEBER AND HIS TIME

1926 Weber, Marianne, *Max Weber. Ein Lebensbild*. Tübingen: J. C. B. Mohr. (Max Weber. A portrait.)

1936 Aron, R. *La Soviologie Allemande contemporaine*. Paris: Alcan. New edition, Paris: Presses Universitaire de France, 1966. (English translation, *German Sociology*. Mary and Thomas Bottomore, translators. London: Heinemann, 1957.)

1935 Brock, W. *An Introduction to Contemporary German Philosophy*. Cambridge: Cambridge University Press.

1938 Weinreich, M. *Max Weber. L'homme et le savant; Etude sur ses idées directrices*. Paris: Vrin.

1959 Hughes, H. Stuart. *Consciousness and Society. The reorientation of European social thought, 1890–1930*. London: MacGibbon & Kee; Paladin, 1974.

1959 Mommsen, W. *Max Weber und die deutsche Politik, 1890–1920*. Tübingen: J. C. B. Mohr.

1960 Bendix, R. *Max Weber. An Intellectual Portrait*. London: Heinemann. (Rev. ed., 1962.)

1963 Baumgarten, E. *Max Weber, Werk und Person*. Tübingen: J. C. B. Mohr.

1965 Loewenstein, K. *Max Webers staatspolitische Auffassungen in der Sicht unserer Zeit*. Frankfurt am Main: Athenäum Verlag. (English translation, *Max Weber's Political Ideas in the Perspective of Our Time*. Massachusetts: University of Massachusetts Press, 1966.)

1966 Freund, J. *La Sociologie de Max Weber*. Paris: Presses Universitaire de France. (English translation, *The Sociology of Max Weber*. Mary Ilford, translator. London: Allen Lane, the Penguin Press, 1968.)

1968 Honigsheim, P. *On Max Weber*. New York: Free Press.

1970 Mitzman, A. *The Iron cage, An Historical Interpretation of Max Weber*. New York: Alfred Knopf.

1971 Dronberger, I. *The Political Thought of Max Weber; in Quest of Statesmanship*. New York: Appleton-Century-Crofts.

1972   Runciman, G. *A Critique of Max Weber's Philosophy of Social Science*. Cambridge: Cambridge University Press.